# Financial Management for Development

**INTRAC NGO Management and Policy Series**

1. *Institutional Development and NGOs in Africa: Policy Perspectives for European Development Agencies* Alan Fowler with Piers Campbell and Brian Pratt

2. *Governance, Democracy and Conditionality: What Role for NGOs?* Edited by Andrew Clayton

3. *Measuring the Process: Guidelines for Evaluating Social Development* David Marsden, Peter Oakley and Brian Pratt

4. *Strengthening the Capacity of NGOs: Cases of Small Enterprise Development Agencies in Africa* Caroline Sahley

5. *NGOs, Civil Society and the State: Building Democracy in Transitional Countries* Edited by Andrew Clayton

6. *Outcomes and Impact: Evaluating Change in Social Development* Peter Oakley, Brian Pratt and Andrew Clayton

7. *Demystifying Organisation Development: Practical Capacity-Building Experiences of African NGOs* Rick James

8. *Direct Funding from a Southern Perspective: Strengthening Civil Society?* INTRAC

9. *Partners in Urban Poverty Alleviation: Urban NGOs in the South* INTRAC

10. *Financial Management for Development: Accounting and Finance for the Non-specialist in Development Organisations* John Cammack

# Financial Management for Development:

## *Accounting and Finance for the Non-specialist in Development Organisations*

John Cammack

INTRAC NGO Management and Policy Series No. 10

An INTRAC Publication

**INTRAC:**
**The International Non-governmental Organisation Training and Research Centre**

**A Summary Description**
INTRAC was set up in 1991 to provide specially designed management, training and research services for NGOs involved in relief and development in the South and dedicated to improving organisational effectiveness and programme performance of Northern NGOs and Southern partners where appropriate. Our goal is to serve NGOs in (i) the exploration of the management, policy and human resource issues affecting their own organisational development, and (ii) the evolution of more effective programmes of institutional development and cooperation.

INTRAC offers the complementary services of:
Training;
Consultancy; and
Research

First published in 1999 in the UK by
INTRAC
PO Box 563
Oxford
OX2 6RZ
United Kingdom

Tel: +44 (0)1865 201851
Fax: +44 (0)1865 201852
e-mail: intrac@gn.apc.org

ISBN 1-897748-52-3

Designed and produced by
Davies Burman Associates
Tel: 01865 343131

Printed in Great Britain by
Antony Rowe Ltd., Chippenham, Wiltshire

# Contents

# Acknowledgements

My thanks are due to those who have encouraged me to write this book and given me ideas for it. This includes the many people who have attended training workshops that I have facilitated and provided me with a chance, maybe unknowingly, to develop some of the main themes contained herein.

Particular thanks are due to those who have read through versions of the text and provided invaluable comments. They are Freda Cammack, Marie Gangi Diaz, Nicola Elliott, William Ogara and Gopal Rao.

I'd also like to thank Susan Barratt and Beth Mwisywa (Carr Stanyer Gitau and Co., Nairobi) for their inputs to the audit chapter. Sightsavers International have been kind enough to give me permission to reproduce some of the questions from their internal control questionnaire.

Special thanks are due to Freda and Stephen for their constant support and encouragement throughout the time of writing this book.

*John Cammack*
Oxford
December 1999

# Introduction

Development organisations range from small community groups to large international donors – for each of them, financial management is important. Good stewardship demands clear accounting and quality financial reporting and management. These skills enable organisations to manage their programmes effectively, to report to stakeholders and donors and to make optimum use of the often limited resources available.

This book is primarily for managers, staff and governing bodies of development organisations who need to understand and interpret financial information. It can also be used as a training resource. Focusing on not-for-profit organisations and illustrated with examples, it examines step by step the main financial systems and accounting statements.

Recognising that the book will be used in a number of countries, the systems and statements examined follow current international practice. Individual currencies have not been included. Development organisations, including non-governmental organisations, are referred to throughout as 'NGOs'. The specialised format for larger charities' own accounting statements which applies in the United Kingdom only, is outside the scope of this book.

Checklists provided in the appendices can be used in reviewing an organisation's financial systems and data. Any technical or unusual terms are shown in bold and included in a comprehensive glossary.

# Chapter 1

## Budgeting

**OBJECTIVES OF THIS CHAPTER**

This chapter examines three stages of the budgeting process – planning, monitoring and reviewing – and provides some key questions with which to analyse this process within an organisation.

Having considered the material and worked through the examples in this chapter, you should be able to:

- explain each stage of the budgeting process – planning, monitoring and reviewing;
- distinguish between a revenue and a capital budget;
- prepare a straightforward budget;
- analyse, and raise questions about a budget statement;
- interpret a statement comparing the budget with actual income and expenditure, and identify questions to ask and action to take;
- assess how well a development organisation's budgeting process is managed.

A **budget** can be defined as *a financial plan of an entity relating to a period of time*. This is a useful definition because it includes planning – budgeting is about planning for the future.

The process of budgeting can be divided into three main areas.

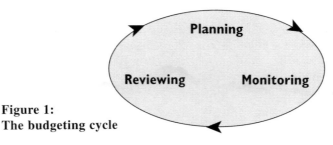

**Figure 1:**
**The budgeting cycle**

*Planning* is the preparation of the budget from the range of data available, within the overall guidelines and longer-term plans of the organisation. Budgeting is about planning **objectives** as well as finance. The first stage of a budget is to decide what needs to be achieved over a particular period. The quality of a budget will depend on its ability to present a clear plan of activities designed to meet organisational objectives.

*Monitoring* the budget, usually month by month, checks that the actual income and expenditure matches the estimates originally set in the budget. This is achieved by producing regular statements which identify the differences between the original budget, and the income or expenditure to date.

*Reviewing* is an ongoing monthly task, but a general review may take place towards the end of each financial year, leading into next year's planning stage. It is an opportunity to identify areas which need to be managed differently.

## BUDGET PLANNING

The starting point for the preparation of a budget is the identification of any **limiting factors**. This recognises what might prevent all the objectives being achieved within the budget period. In not-for-profit organisations with social objectives, the limiting factor may be the amount of cash or human and other resources available. The budget should be realistic but must be prepared with these limitations in mind, together with other organisational guidelines, for example, growth or a reduced level of operation.

There are a number of reasons for preparing budgets, including to:
- plan and co-ordinate activities;
- calculate the estimated income and expenditure;
- communicate the plans;
- motivate staff to achieve the objectives;
- assist in the monitoring and evaluation of performance.

### TYPES OF BUDGET

The main budget statement is sometimes described as a **revenue budget**. This includes ongoing income and expenditure for a particular period of time – often one year. Excluded from this may be items which will last for longer than a year, for example vehicles, equipment and computers.

An organisation may also prepare a **capital budget**. This estimates the cost of these longer-term items, and identifies where the money will come from to fund them.

**Non-governmental organisations** and other **development organisations** (referred to throughout this book as 'NGOs') may include capital and revenue items in one statement, and simply call it *the budget!*

## CALCULATING COSTS

Each item in the budget needs to be carefully considered, and a record kept of how its figure is calculated. Some items are straightforward. The yearly 'rent of premises' figure, for example, may simply be the amount to be paid each month multiplied by 12.

Other items might be more complicated. They may need estimates from suppliers, the previous year's details of, for example, costs for electricity plus an increase for **inflation**, or annual salary figures plus any agreed increases.

A training budget, for example, may need to be calculated in detail to include all or some of the information shown in Figure 2.

---

Trainer's fees and expenses
Fees for invited speakers
Cost of administrative support (if not included elsewhere in the budget)
Accommodation costs (if a residential course) for participants and trainer
Costs of catering and food
Travel costs – for trainer, participants and administrative staff
Photocopying of training materials
Hire of training venue
Hire of equipment needed
Hire of audio-visual materials (for example, videos)
Cost of participants' time (even if not included in the training budget, this
                    is an interesting figure with which to calculate
                    the cost-effectiveness of training)
Fees received from course participants
Grants towards the cost of training
Any other income (for example from sale of materials, or sponsorship)

---

**Figure 2: Possible expenditure and income items of a training budget**

A further process would be to cost the training activity. This may be derived by taking the budgeted expenditure together with any other hidden costs not in the budget (for example costs of electricity, cleaning of the premises), and divide this total by the number of participant days. The result gives the cost per participant per day and can be used as the basis for assessing any fee chargeable or preparing a funding proposal.

It may also be necessary to identify the number of courses to be run during the year and the minimum number of participants necessary to cover costs. It is important to consider whether an external body could undertake the training at a lower cost than internal trainers.

Estimated income and expenditure for training will then need to be totalled and included in the budget statement. All this detailed work may result in an entry of just one or two lines in the final budget statement.

## BUDGETING FOR INCOME

Budgets at an organisational level should always include **income** as well as **expenditure**. NGOs are often unsure whether to include details of income for which grant applications have been made, but are still not approved. In this situation, all confirmed income should be included and any amounts not yet approved included as 'unconfirmed grants'. When compiling the budget, it is useful to identify the precise status of any grant applications, and to state the sources approached for funding.

If grant applications have not been approved prior to the start of the period, the programme may need to be delayed or the whole budget recalculated.

## BUDGETS AND PRICE INCREASES

Budgets are prepared in advance and there are likely to be price increases between the time of preparation and the time when the amount is spent or received. These increases are often referred to as **inflation**.

There are no easy solutions to this, but the amounts used in the budget – both for expenditure and income – should include their estimated values when they will be paid or received. For example:

- **Items to be purchased at a fixed price**
  If an estimate has been agreed with a supplier, this price should be fixed, and should be included as such in the budget.
- **Salaries**
  Salaries may be difficult to estimate if they are likely to increase in line with the general level of price increases. You can only include your best estimate.
- **Items that are likely to increase in price**
  If the amount of the increase is unknown, the rate of past increases may be

a guide. Governments may forecast what the level of price increases may be. This should however be used with care, as most governments will be over-optimistic! It is better to use your own best estimate.

- **Increase in income**

  If inflation is forecast, this should also be reflected in an increase in income – particularly items such as 'fees and charges' which can be decided by the organisation itself.

At a time of inflation, it is necessary to encourage people who owe money to pay quickly, to avoid financial loss. Organisations may decide not to allow **credit** in these circumstances.

Calculations for an inflationary effect in the budget should be carefully documented and kept. This is especially important if the calculations are later found to be wrong! **Donors** working with NGOs will often consider providing a supplementary grant to cover inflation, *but only if the original budget calculations can be produced together with details of what has happened to change it.*

## DEPRECIATION AND BUDGETS

**Depreciation** is an estimation of the *loss in value* of an item such as a vehicle, computer, or equipment, during the period of the budget. An explanation of the methods of calculating depreciation is included in Chapter 6.

Although depreciation is not always included in an NGO's budget, it does however provide a sound approach to financial management and will be included in the budget planning example below.

## BUDGET PLANNING AND REPORTING BACK TO DONORS

Many donors will require a report at the end of the budget period on how their money has been spent.

A key requirement in preparing a budget proposal for a donor is that the NGO will be able to report back *in the same format* as the budget. To enable this to happen, changes may be needed to the draft budget and to the accounting system itself. An example might be to introduce a new section of headings in the accounting system to cover items in the programme being funded. The aim is to be consistent in both budget and accounting headings.

If this is not thought through at the planning stage, it can cause considerable work in trying to account for money spent, and at worst, having to repay some of the funds because they cannot be accounted for. If money has to be repaid, it can influence the donor's perception of the NGO's credibility. This in turn, may affect future funding applications.

If many different donors are involved in funding, there would ideally be one financial report acceptable to all. However, when donors' requirements are different, it is at the planning stage – before any money is requested – that it is necessary to consider whether the NGO's accounting system is capable of producing the information required by each donor.

When a large donation is received and additional accounting is required, it is worth considering whether the current *level* of accounting skills is sufficient for the organisation. If in doubt, it is worth consulting a qualified **accountant** at this stage to prevent difficulties arising later.

## 'WHAT IF' BUDGETS

Preparing a budget means taking a view of what the income and expenditure will be. This can be difficult for development organisations because the amount of income can be so uncertain. Therefore, whilst preparing a main **working budget** version of the revenue budget – what is realistically expected to happen – many organisations prepare for 'what if' scenarios. 'What if' scenarios are in fact a method of putting together plans in case the unexpected happens. This shows good forward planning on behalf of the organisation's management. These 'additional' budgets are sometimes described as:

- a **survival budget**. The minimum required to keep existing programmes going.
- a **guaranteed budget**. The budget based on income guaranteed at the time the budget is planned.
- an **optimal budget**. The programme that would be undertaken given that the most favourable amount of funding were available.

## BUDGET PLANNING EXAMPLE

The following example shows information that is likely to be needed when preparing an NGO's budget. For example:
- the current year's budget;
- the latest statement comparing the budget with actual income and expenditure for the current year;
- details of costs for the following year, for example price increases, salary

agreements;
* figures for any depreciation to be charged in the following year.

---

*The case study used throughout is the Lomtaka Health Care Centre. It is a clinic staffed by a director, doctors, nurses and administrative personnel. The Centre is supported by an annual grant from the Department of Health and other grants from international non-governmental organisations. Each year the Centre compiles a separate revenue and a capital budget. The Centre insists that expenditure equals income in both budgets.*

*The financial year runs from January to December. The Lomtaka Centre's details are from the first two years of its existence and any examples of actual documents are shown in the text with a shaded background. Where relevant, the years are distinguished as year 1 or year 2.*

*The Lomtaka Health Care Centre is fictitious.*

---

**Page 1 of the example** shows the revenue and capital budget compared with the actual income and expenditure for the first 10 months of year 1 (the latest available at the time the next year's budget is prepared). It includes the following columns:

* year 1's annual budget (12 months) – shown for information only;
* the budget for the first 10 months of year 1 (January to October);
* actual income and expenditure for the same 10-month period;
* the **variance** (or difference between the budget, and actual income and expenditure figures) over the 10-month period;
* a percentage variance column. This helps to identify more clearly, significant changes from the budget. The brackets in the variance columns indicate that actual income is less than in the budget, and that actual expenditure is more than expected in the budget.

**Page 2 of the example** provides information gathered for the following financial year (year 2).

**Page 3 of the example** compiles the budget for the following financial year (year 2).

## BUDGET PLANNING EXAMPLE (page 1)

### REVENUE BUDGET AND ACTUAL STATEMENT FOR THE LOMTAKA HEALTH CARE CENTRE FROM JANUARY TO OCTOBER (YEAR 1)

| | Annual Budget 12 months | Budget (Jan–Oct) 10 months | Actual (Jan–Oct) 10 months | Variance 10 months | % Variance 10 months |
|---|---|---|---|---|---|
| **INCOME** | | | | | |
| Grant from WEV | 100,000 | 100,000 | 100,000 | - | - |
| Grant from Donoraid | 250,000 | 250,000 | 150,000 | (100,000) | (40%)* |
| Department of Health | 350,000 | 300,000 | 260,000 | (40,000) | (13%) |
| Fees and charges | 124,000 | 100,000 | 102,680 | 2,680 | 3% |
| Other income | - | - | 2,790 | 2,790 | - |
| *Total income* | *824,000* | *750,000* | *615,470* | *(134,530)* | *(18%)* |
| **EXPENDITURE** | | | | | |
| Salaries | 467,130 | 389,280 | 426,090 | (36,810) | (9%) |
| Rent of premises | 96,000 | 80,000 | 80,000 | - | - |
| Purchase of drugs | 132,000 | 110,000 | 73,970 | 36,030 | 33% |
| Medical supplies | 64,560 | 53,800 | 42,965 | 10,835 | 20% |
| Electricity | 12,840 | 10,700 | 10,465 | 235 | 2% |
| Travelling expenses | 20,070 | 15,300 | 16,143 | (843) | (6%) |
| Training programme | 5,000 | 5,000 | 4,807 | 193 | 4% |
| Office costs (including audit) | 11,400 | 9,500 | 8,956 | 544 | 6% |
| Depreciation | 15,000 | 12,500 | - | 12,500 | 100% |
| *Total expenditure* | *824,000* | *686,080* | *663,396* | *22,684* | *3%* |

- \* variance % calculated as: $(100,000 \div 250,000) \times 100 = 40\%$.
- variance %s are rounded to the nearest whole number.
- ( ) indicates a negative variance (actual income lower than the budget *or* actual expenditure higher than the budget).

### CAPITAL BUDGET AND ACTUAL STATEMENT FOR THE LOMTAKA HEALTH CARE CENTRE FROM JANUARY TO OCTOBER (YEAR 1)

| | Annual Budget 12 months | Budget (Jan–Oct) 10 months | Actual (Jan–Oct) 10 months | Variance 10 months | % Variance 10 months |
|---|---|---|---|---|---|
| **INCOME** | | | | | |
| Department of Health | 45,000 | 45,000 | 45,000 | - | - |
| **EXPENDITURE** | | | | | |
| Vehicle | 15,000 | 15,000 | 15,298 | (298) | (2%) |
| Equipment | 30,000 | 30,000 | 30,198 | (198) | (1%) |

## BUDGET PLANNING EXAMPLE (page 2)

### INFORMATION ABOUT YEAR 2

1. Grants for year 2: WEV is to remain at 100,000.00, and Donoraid is to increase to 300,000.00.

2. The Department of Health is to increase its contribution to 450,000.00.

3. The fees and charges budget for year 1 has been calculated as 139,080.00 in year 2.

4. Salaries are expected to be as follows:

   3 staff at 80,000.00 per year      4 staff at 30,000.00 per year
   2 staff at 45,000.00 per year      2 staff at 20,000.00 per year
   (Total salaries, excluding employment tax: 490,000.00)

   All staff will be subject to an 8% employment tax payable from the Centre's budget.

5. Rent will be increased to 10,000.00 per month in year 2.

6. The year 1 budget for drugs, medical supplies, electricity and office costs will increase by 10% in year 2.

7. Travelling expenses, including the running costs of the new vehicles, are expected to be 30,000.00 in year 2.

8. A training programme is planned for year 2. 20,880.00 should be included for this, plus another 5,000.00 for other training. If the budget cannot be balanced, it has been agreed that part of the training will be cancelled.

9. The Centre wishes to buy new vehicles in the middle of year 2, to improve the health care in remote areas. These are estimated to cost 75,000.00. The Department of Health has agreed to fund the actual capital cost, but the Centre must include the depreciation of the vehicles in its annual revenue budget from year 2 onwards. In year 2 this is estimated to be 40,000.00.

   Depreciation should also be included in the year 2 budget, for the vehicle and equipment already purchased in year 1. In year 2 it is estimated to be 10,000.00.

**BUDGET PLANNING EXAMPLE (page 3)**

**THE BUDGET FOR YEAR 2**

The Centre has decided that the 'training programme' will be reduced in scale, to enable the revenue budget to balance. (Details of all calculations are shown in brackets).

**LOMTAKA  HEALTH CARE CENTRE**
**REVENUE BUDGET 1 JANUARY TO 31 DECEMBER (YEAR 2)**

|  | Amount 12 months |  |
|---|---|---|
| **INCOME** | | |
| Grant from WEV (note 1) | 100,000 | |
| Grant from Donoraid (note 1) | 300,000 | |
| Department of Health (note 2) | 450,000 | |
| Fees and charges (note 3) | 139,080 | |
| *Total income* | *989,080* | |
| | | |
| **EXPENDITURE** | | |
| Salaries (note 4: 490,000 + 8% employment tax) | 529,200 | |
| Rent of premises (note 5: 10,000 x 12 months) | 120,000 | |
| Purchase of drugs (note 6: 132,000 + 10%) | 145,200 | |
| Medical supplies (note 6: 64,560 + 10%) | 71,016 | |
| Electricity (note 6: 12,840 + 10%) | 14,124 | |
| Travelling expenses (note 7) | 30,000 | |
| Training programme (note 8: 20,880 + 5,000 - 8,880) | 17,000 | (reduction of 8,880.00 to balance the budget) |
| Office costs (including audit) (note 6: 11,400 + 10%) | 12,540 | |
| Depreciation  (note 9: 40,000 + 10,000) | 50,000 | |
| *Total expenditure* | *989,080* | |

**CAPITAL BUDGET 1 JANUARY TO 31 DECEMBER (YEAR 2)**

|  | Amount 12 months |
|---|---|
| **INCOME** | |
| Department of Health (note 9) | 75,000 |
| | |
| **EXPENDITURE** | |
| Purchase of vehicles (note 9) | 75,000 |

## KEY POINTS FROM THE BUDGET PLANNING EXAMPLE

Budget users may often be interested in interpreting the information in the budget rather than compiling it. This information may be used to help assess the ability of an NGO to achieve its objectives. The user can gain further information by asking questions. Questions to ask the Lomtaka Centre would include for example:

- Will the grants from the Department of Health and other donors be received in full?
- Will the increased fees and charges actually be received?
- What is the forecast rate of inflation? How close is it to the increases suggested?
- Will drugs and medical supplies be purchased with foreign currency? If so, will the estimated price increases be correct?
- Are there other costs relating to the new vehicles? For example, freight or import duties.
- How important is the training? What will the effects be to staff and patients of the reduction in the scale of the training programme? Could, or should this reduction be separately funded?
- Will the Lomtaka Centre be able to keep within the budget?
- Who will monitor the budget? What documentation will be produced to help with this?

# BUDGET MONITORING

Budget monitoring is used to measure how closely an organisation is meeting its objectives in terms of its finances and its programme. Comparisons of actual income and expenditure with the budgeted figures are required on a regular basis to determine if the income and expenditure is under or over what was expected, or about the same. A **budget and actual statement** (also known as a **financial report, variance report** and by many other names!) is the document produced to identify these differences or **variances**. It will usually be produced monthly or quarterly.

Preparing the statement and comparing the figures provides an opportunity to take the appropriate action to ensure that the objectives will be achieved. It is important that someone examines these figures and takes any corrective action as soon as possible after the end of the period.

An excellent way of analysing the statement is for the manager of the organisation or programme, with the help of finance staff, to add notes to the budget and actual statement to explain differences and explain any action taken. This shows that the statement is being regularly monitored.

If a **donor** then receives such an annotated budget and actual statement, the donor's role may be to ensure that the monitoring process and corrective action have taken place, rather than having to examine the statement itself in detail.

## ADJUSTMENTS TO THE BUDGET AND ACTUAL STATEMENTS

The accounting information for a particular period should include expenditure incurred, or income earned during that period. This means that amounts *due* for activities *in the particular period* not received or not paid until the following period, should still be included in the accounts *for that period*.

Accountants could adjust the accounts to comply with this rule whenever financial information is produced, but this would take an enormous amount of time. Adjustments are therefore made at the end of the financial year and sometimes quarterly and half-yearly. These adjustments are referred to as **accruals** and **prepayments**. (These terms are explained in more detail in Chapter 6.)

An example of how this is achieved can be seen in the 'rent of premises' item from the budget and actual statement for the Lomtaka Centre (page 10), shown in Figure 3.

| | Annual Budget 12 months | Budget (Jan–Oct) 10 months | Actual (Jan–Oct) 10 months | Variance 10 months | % Variance 10 months |
|---|---|---|---|---|---|
| Rent of premises | 96,000 | 80,000 | 80,000 | - | - |

**Figure 3: Extract of 'rent of premises' from the Lomtaka Centre's budget and actual statement**

The budget and actual figures from January to October are both shown as 80,000.00, that is 8,000.00 per month. It *may* be that the actual rent has only been *paid* up to September (9 months x 8,000.00 = 72,000.00), but that the figure has been adjusted for what *should* have been paid (10 months x 8,000.00 = 80,000.00) to give a true comparison with the budget. If this has happened, it would be described as 'an accrual adjustment'.

The first question to ask in examining a budget and actual statement is, therefore, whether it has been adjusted for accruals and prepayments. If not, this must be taken into account when using the document, and a revised figure calculated that is comparable with the budgeted amount.

If the statement has been adjusted, it is safe to take the figures as comparing 'like with like'.

## BUDGET MONITORING EXAMPLE

The following example uses the statement prepared in the budget planning example for year 2 (page 12). It compares this with the actual income and expenditure of the Lomtaka Centre for the period January to October (year 2), that is the first ten months of year 2.

### BUDGET MONITORING EXAMPLE

#### REVENUE BUDGET AND ACTUAL STATEMENT FOR THE LOMTAKA HEALTH CARE CENTRE FROM JANUARY TO OCTOBER (YEAR 2)

|  | Annual Budget 12 months | Budget (Jan–Oct) 10 months | Actual (Jan–Oct) 10 months | Variance 10 months | % Variance 10 months |
|---|---|---|---|---|---|
| **INCOME** | | | | | |
| Grant from WEV | 100,000 | 100,000 | 100,000 | - | - |
| Grant from Donoraid | 300,000 | 300,000 | 150,000 | (150,000) | (50%)* |
| Department of Health | 450,000 | 300,000 | 300,000 | - | - |
| Fees and charges | 139,080 | 115,900 | 106,290 | (9,610) | (8%) |
| Other income | - | - | 10,374 | 10,374 | - |
| *Total income* | *989,080* | *815,900* | *666,664* | *(149,236)* | *(18%)* |
| **EXPENDITURE** | | | | | |
| Salaries | 529,200 | 441,000 | 463,084 | (22,084) | (5%) |
| Rent of premises | 120,000 | 100,000 | 100,000 | - | - |
| Purchase of drugs | 145,200 | 108,900 | 72,592 | 36,308 | 33% |
| Medical supplies | 71,016 | 59,180 | 52,278 | 6,902 | 12% |
| Electricity | 14,124 | 11,770 | 12,232 | (462) | (4%) |
| Travelling expenses | 30,000 | 25,000 | 21,857 | 3,143 | 13% |
| Training programme | 17,000 | 16,200 | 13,931 | 2,269 | 14% |
| Office costs (including audit) | 12,540 | 10,450 | 10,234 | 216 | 2% |
| Depreciation | 50,000 | 41,667 | - | 41,667 | 100% |
| *Total expenditure* | *989,080* | *814,167* | *746,208* | *67,959* | *8%* |

- * variance % calculated as: $(150,000 \div 300,000) \times 100 = 50\%$.
- variance %s are rounded to the nearest whole number.
- ( ) indicates a negative variance (actual income lower than the budget *or* actual expenditure higher than the budget).

## CAPITAL BUDGET AND ACTUAL STATEMENT FOR THE LOMTAKA HEALTH CARE CENTRE FROM JANUARY TO OCTOBER (YEAR 2)

| | Annual Budget 12 months | Budget (Jan–Oct) 10 months | Actual (Jan–Oct) 10 months | Variance 10 months | % Variance 10 months |
|---|---|---|---|---|---|
| **INCOME** | | | | | |
| Department of Health | 75,000 | 75,000 | 66,804 | (8,196) | (11%) |
| | | | | | |
| **EXPENDITURE** | | | | | |
| Vehicles | 75,000 | 75,000 | 66,804 | 8,196 | 11% |

## KEY POINTS FROM THE BUDGET MONITORING EXAMPLE

Most users of budget and actual statements interpret the information by asking further questions. In the Lomtaka example, such questions might include:

- Have the 'actual' figures been adjusted for accruals and prepayments? If they have, it is safe to compare the figures as representing 'like with like'.
- Is the accounting system up to date? If not, some of the 'actual' figures may have been estimated (for comparison purposes), which may mean the information is less accurate.
- The Donoraid payment is late! When will this arrive and does the Lomtaka Centre have enough cash to pay its debts?
- Fees and charges are less than the budget. Why is there a difference? 'Other income' appears to cover the difference. What is the 'other income' and why was it not included in the original budget?
- Salaries are considerably over budget. Why is this? Have additional staff been employed and where will the money come from to pay for this? It is usually possible to estimate the salaries budget reasonably accurately.
- Purchase of drugs is below budget. There may be supply difficulties or an invoice outstanding (adjusting for accruals would have corrected this).
- All other costs, except electricity, are below budget. Has the number of patients remained as expected? If not, why are the salaries so high?
- Depreciation has not yet been charged, so the actual expenditure and variance shows a false picture. This is not unusual! Accountants often include the depreciation figure as a single item at the end of the year. Will it be similar to the estimated amount when it actually appears?
- How has the annual budget been spread over the months? Has the total been

divided by twelve months or has the amount been allocated in the months in which it will be received or paid. For example if the main training event was in June it would be sensible to include most of the budget figure in that month rather than spread it over the full twelve months.

The Lomtaka Centre could also show the number of patients expected and treated during this period (rather like a 'patient budget'!). This may help to interpret the data.

As mentioned already, it is helpful if the budget and actual statement contains notes giving reasons for the variances. The NGO has to think through the reasons to be able to write the notes. It also provides explanations to others using the statements (for example donors). An example of this is shown below:

---

**NOTES TO ACCOMPANY THE BUDGET MONITORING EXAMPLE**

1. The 150,000.00 from Donoraid is expected to arrive in late November.
2. It has been decided by the governing body that *fees and charges* cannot be increased by as much as planned during this year. The position will be reviewed before the next financial year begins.
3. *Other income* includes donations and the proceeds of small fund-raising events.
4. An additional member of staff has been appointed from March to October.
5. The original budget for *purchase of drugs* is thought to have been too high. There is an invoice outstanding (not included in the actual) at 31 October for 13,392.00 which relates to September.
6. Depreciation for the whole year will be charged in December. It is expected to be close to the budgeted figure.

---

The notes here give explanations for the larger variances in the budget and actual statement. Some questions which a user of the statement may want to ask however are still unanswered (for example, *why* has the additional member of staff been appointed and *how much* is the over-budgeting for purchase of drugs?).

The final, and most important stage of monitoring a budget is to determine the action needed from the information available. There may be no action to take or it may be necessary, for example, to reduce the organisation's activity level in order to stay within the budget. Sometimes it is possible to transfer part of the budget from one item to another. This is described as **virement**. Usually permission must be obtained to do this from a senior manager or a donor.

# BUDGET REVIEWING

The budget review takes place towards the end of the financial year, prior to planning the following year's budget. It provides an opportunity to:

- evaluate effectiveness of the programme objectives;
- learn from past experience and decide how to make use of this knowledge;
- implement any organisational policy changes;
- identify different ways of performing the same task;
- examine alternative methods of budgeting, for example **zero-based budgeting**. This  principle is that each year's budget should be based on the planned activities for that year. Initially there is no commitment to spend on any item. Zero-based budgeting helps to *realign* the budget if the base figures have, over a period, moved away from the original objectives of the organisation. This method of budgeting is in contrast to using last year's figures and adjusting by an agreed percentage.

# THE BUDGET PROCESS WITHIN AN ORGANISATION

The budget process varies considerably from one organisation to another. The following questions give a useful framework from which to assess how well this process is managed.

### 1.  HOW MUCH  INVOLVEMENT?

Staff participation in the budget process is desirable from both a management and a financial viewpoint. With such involvement, motivation and communication may improve and staff are more likely to feel that the organisation's objectives are relevant to their own work.

### 2.  HOW WELL CO-ORDINATED AND COMMUNICATED?

The budget process involves co-ordinating the different parts of the budget to make sure that income is sufficient to cover expenditure. The more staff participate in the process, the more they will work towards meeting budget targets. Good communication of the budget is vital in order that staff know what is required of them.

### 3.  HOW MUCH DOES THE PAST DICTATE THE FUTURE?

The budget must reflect current organisational aspirations. The previous year's figures can be a guide, but they too may have been based on previous years. The objectives now may not be the same as they were a few years ago.

## 4. IS ANY EXCESS INCLUDED?

The process of budget planning may allow unnecessary amounts of expenditure to be included. For example an item for air travel might be included instead of a more cost-effective method of travel. How good is the system for identifying what should be included?

## 5. HOW GOOD IS THE ACCOUNTING?

Budget preparation and monitoring will be more accurate if the accounting on which it is based is sound. If accounting errors occur (for example, an item has been charged to the wrong account heading), the actual expenditure when compared with the budget becomes less useful as a means of monitoring.

## 6. HOW ENCOURAGING ARE THE FINANCIAL STAFF?

A good relationship between financial and non-financial staff will maximise the benefits of the accounting system. Where financial staff adopt an 'enabling' rather than a 'policing' role, it encourages a more responsive attitude both to budgeting and to accounting in general.

## 7. ARE THERE OTHER WAYS OF ACHIEVING THE OBJECTIVES?

It is important to link planning and objective setting to the whole budget process. Budgeting is not undertaken for its own sake! The budget review and planning stages are an appropriate point to look again at all the organisation's activities to see if there are more efficient or effective ways of working.

# Chapter 2

## Cash Budgets
## (Cash Flow Forcasts)

---

**OBJECTIVES OF THIS CHAPTER**

The technique of cash budgeting is explained and an example prepared. The key points of this example are then highlighted.

Having considered the material and worked through the example in this chapter, you should be able to:

- describe what is meant by a cash budget;
- list the stages in compiling one;
- prepare a simple cash budget;
- analyse a cash budget and advise on ways an NGO could improve its cash management.

---

A **cash budget** (also called a **cash flow forecast**) is a technique for estimating the pattern in which money will come in to and go out of an organisation over a period of time.

It predicts the flow of money whether in cash or through the bank and enables the organisation to see in advance, if there are months when there will be insufficient money to pay its debts. If this is so, appropriate action can be taken.

A similar process may be taken with personal finances in order to decide what money is coming in to and going out of a bank account, and when there will be sufficient funds available to pay a bill! For individuals, it is possible to remember most of this information, but for an organisation there are so many activities that it is essential to write it down in a structured way.

A cash budget is always an excellent method of managing cash for an ongoing group or organisation – whatever its size. It is essential to prepare a cash budget at the start of any new venture.

PERIOD:

CASH BUDGET FOR

Period:

Receipts:

*TOTAL RECEIPTS (1)*

**Payments:**

*TOTAL PAYMENTS (2)*
OPENING CASH/BANK BALANCE
+ TOTAL RECEIPTS (1)
- TOTAL PAYMENTS (2)
**CLOSING CASH/BANK BALANCE**

**Figure 4: Outline format for use in preparing a cash budget (cash flow forecast)**

# PREPARATION OF A CASH BUDGET

The first step in preparing a cash budget is to obtain a copy of the organisation's budget (capital *and* revenue) for the period concerned. This, together with details of *when* money will come in and go out over the period (or the best estimate of when), gives the basis of the cash budget.

An outline cash budget must then be completed. A suggested format is illustrated in Figure 4. It shows the periods, possibly months along the top of the page and the types of money coming in (**receipts**) and going out (**payments**) listed down the left side. The estimated receipts and payments must be entered, item by item, for each period. This will be *when the receipt or payment will actually be made* – even if the amount is *due* in a previous or future period.

The **opening balance** represents an estimate of the total amount of money that will be held in cash and in the bank account at the start of the period. The opening balance for a new organisation will be nil. The anticipated closing cash and bank balance for each month is estimated by taking the opening balance *plus* the total receipts for that month and *less* the total payments. The estimated closing balance of, for example January, then becomes the estimated opening balance for February.

Some months will show an overdrawn estimated closing balance. The cash budget must then be examined to see if any receipt could be received earlier, or any payment made later. If there are still months with overdrawn estimated closing balances, these months must be covered by a temporary loan or bank overdraft, arranged *in advance*.

If there are months with a substantial cash/bank balance in hand, the possibility of investing the surplus amount on a short-term basis (for example in a bank **deposit account**) could be considered. Care must however be taken with donated money, as some donors do not allow their money to be invested!

If the cash budget shows the organisation is constantly overdrawn, it may be that the proposed activity or organisation is not financially viable and, unless additional funding is obtained it will not be advisable to go ahead.

The cash budget should be updated throughout the period, as actual information becomes available.

## CASH BUDGET EXAMPLE

**Page 1 of the example** shows the capital and revenue budgets for year 2, constructed in Chapter 1.

**Page 2 of the example** gives the information gathered about when the amounts in the budget will be received or paid.

**Page 3 of the example** puts together a cash budget for the first six months of year 2.

## CASH BUDGET EXAMPLE (page 1)

### BUDGET INFORMATION

A cash budget is constructed using the Lomtaka Health Care Centre capital and revenue budgets for year 2 as a starting point. This is compiled in Chapter 1 and reproduced below.

### REVENUE BUDGET 1 JANUARY TO 31 DECEMBER (YEAR 2)

|  | Amount 12 months |
|---|---|
| **INCOME** | |
| Grant from WEV | 100,000 |
| Grant from Donoraid | 300,000 |
| Department of Health | 450,000 |
| Fees and charges | 139,080 |
| *Total income* | *989,080* |
| **EXPENDITURE** | |
| Salaries | 529,200 |
| Rent of premises | 120,000 |
| Purchase of drugs | 145,200 |
| Medical supplies | 71,016 |
| Electricity | 14,124 |
| Travelling expenses | 30,000 |
| Training programme | 17,000 |
| Office costs (including audit) | 12,540 |
| Depreciation | 50,000 |
| *Total expenditure* | *989,080* |

### CAPITAL BUDGET 1 JANUARY TO 31 DECEMBER (YEAR 2)

|  | Amount 12 months |
|---|---|
| **INCOME** | |
| Department of Health | 75,000 |
| **EXPENDITURE** | |
| Vehicles | 75,000 |

# CASH BUDGET EXAMPLE (page 2)

## FURTHER INFORMATION

The following is the 'best estimate' of when items will be received or paid, made before the start of year 2. This information has been compiled after consulting the Centre's staff. The budget shown on the next page covers the first six months of year 2 only.

1. The grant from WEV will be received in May and November (50,000.00 each).

2. Donoraid's grant will be received in April and October (150,000.00 each).

3. The Department of Health's grant will be paid in January, May and October (150,000.00 each). The 75,000.00 income for the vehicle in the capital budget will be received in July.

4. Fees and charges will be received evenly throughout the year.

5. The salaries, rent, medical supplies, travelling expenses and office costs will all be paid evenly throughout the year. The total budget therefore needs to be divided by twelve to obtain the monthly amount.

6. The purchase of drugs will be in four equal instalments of 36,300.00, paid in January, April, July and October.

7. Electricity will be paid quarterly in arrears, in March, June, September and December. A quarter of the total for each payment (3,531.00), has been assumed.

8. The training programme expenditure will include 12,000.00 in February for a major conference and 5,000.00, which will be spent evenly throughout the 12 months of the year.

9. The new vehicles are expected to be purchased in July (75,000.00).

10. Depreciation should *not* be included as it does not involve cash coming in or going out.

11. The opening cash/bank balance at 1 January is estimated to be 30,000.00.

## CASH BUDGET EXAMPLE (page 3)

### CASH BUDGET FOR LOMTAKA HEALTH CARE CENTRE
### PERIOD: JANUARY – JUNE, YEAR 2

| Period: | JAN | FEB | MAR | APR | MAY | JUN |
|---|---|---|---|---|---|---|
| **Receipts:** | | | | | | |
| Grant from WEV | | | | | 50,000 | |
| Grant from Donoraid | | | | 150,000 | | |
| Department of Health – revenue | 150,000 | | | | 150,000 | |
| Department of Health – capital | | | | | | |
| Fees and Charges | 11,590 | 11,590 | 11,590 | 11,590 | 11,590 | 11,590 |
| | | | | | | |
| ***TOTAL RECEIPTS (1)*** | *161,590* | *11,590* | *11,590* | *161,590* | *211,590* | *11,590* |
| | | | | | | |
| **Payments:** | | | | | | |
| Salaries | 44,100 | 44,100 | 44,100 | 44,100 | 44,100 | 44,100 |
| Rent of premises | 10,000 | 10,000 | 10,000 | 10,000 | 10,000 | 10,000 |
| Purchase of drugs | 36,300 | | | 36,300 | | |
| Medical supplies | 5,918 | 5,918 | 5,918 | 5,918 | 5,918 | 5,918 |
| Electricity | | | 3,531 | | | 3,531 |
| Travelling expenses | 2,500 | 2,500 | 2,500 | 2,500 | 2,500 | 2,500 |
| Training programme | 417 | 12,417 | 417 | 417 | 417 | 417 |
| Office costs (including audit) | 1,045 | 1,045 | 1,045 | 1,045 | 1,045 | 1,045 |
| Vehicles (capital budget) | | | | | | |
| | | | | | | |
| ***TOTAL PAYMENTS (2)*** | *100,280* | *75,980* | *67,511* | *100,280* | *63,980* | *67,511* |
| | | | | | | |
| OPENING CASH/BANK BALANCE | 30,000 | 91,310 | 26,920 | (29,001) | 32,309 | 179,919 |
| + TOTAL RECEIPTS (1) | 161,590 | 11,590 | 11,590 | 161,590 | 211,590 | 11,590 |
| - TOTAL PAYMENTS (2) | 100,280 | 75,980 | 67,511 | 100,280 | 63,980 | 67,511 |
| **CLOSING CASH/BANK BALANCE** | **91,310** | **26,920** | **(29,001)** | **32,309** | **179,919** | **123,998** |

( ) indicates that the amount is overdrawn

## KEY POINTS FROM THE CASH BUDGET EXAMPLE

The information in this example highlights the following points:

- The Centre will run out of money temporarily in March.
- If Donoraid could be persuaded to pay its grant a month earlier, it would prevent a shortage in March.
- If this is not possible, the other donors could be approached for earlier payment.
- The cash budget gives a structured way of identifying any payments that could be delayed. The purchase of drugs is the only significant amount (other than salaries and rent) that could be delayed. Is it possible to delay payment or could drugs be purchased monthly instead of quarterly?
- If nothing can be altered, it will be necessary to arrange a temporary loan or bank overdraft for March. If not resolved, the overdrawn situation may result in salaries not being paid at the end of March.
- The cash budget indicates months when there are likely to be surplus funds. It may be possible to invest these amounts and gain interest. Any interest expected should be shown as a receipt in the cash budget.

Items from the revenue *and* capital budget are both included in the one cash budget as it is listing money coming in to and going out of the same cash and bank accounts. Depreciation and other **book-keeping adjustments** (see Chapter 6) however should *not* be included in a cash budget.

The information to complete the second six months' cash budget for the Lomtaka Centre is shown in the example. Try and complete it for practice! The 'closing cash/bank balance' at the end of December should come to 30,000.00.

# UPDATING THE CASH BUDGET

When a cash budget has been prepared, it is important to update it each month. The adjustments can be made manually or with a computer spreadsheet package.

When the actual information is available for January, for example, the cash budget figures should be altered to become actual figures. These amendments will then be reflected in future months' closing balances and a different picture may emerge. This is the point at which to add on a further month's cash budget, review the situation for the forthcoming months and take any necessary action.

Good management of the cash budget is essential to avoid cash shortages. *Do not forget that the figures are estimates.* As more up-to-date information becomes available, always amend the figures accordingly!

# INFLATION AND CASH BUDGETS

In countries with a high rate of **inflation**, cash budgets and indeed budgets themselves must be adjusted to reflect the estimated price increases. Inflation may mean it is less appropriate to divide the total amount in the budget by twelve to obtain the monthly receipt or payment figure. The figures in the later months of the year may represent a higher proportion of the budget.

A high rate of inflation makes a cash budget less accurate, but it can still be a useful tool in cash management.

# CASH BUDGETS AND COMPUTER SPREADSHEETS

With access to a computer spreadsheet, cash budgets become much easier to construct and keep up to date. This is because the spreadsheet programme will do a lot of the mathematical work!

# Chapter 3

## Accounting Records and the Receipts and Payments Account

---

**OBJECTIVES OF THIS CHAPTER**

This chapter aims to identify the basic accounting records, and examine the preparation of a bank reconciliation statement. An example of a receipts and payments account, the most straightforward accounting statement, is included.

Having considered the material and worked through the examples in this chapter, you should be able to:

- describe the accounting records used by most organisations;
- list the steps needed to prepare a bank reconciliation;
- prepare a simple bank reconciliation, using cash book and bank statement data;
- recognise a receipts and payments account;
- explain the strengths and weaknesses of a receipts and payments account.

---

The documents used to record financial transactions will be similar throughout the world. The information may be kept in individual books or files often called the manual system, or as a computerised system. When a computerised system is used, some manual records will also be kept to provide additional information.

The records, in whichever form, are referred to as the **books of account** (or simply **'the books'**).

## BASIC ACCOUNTING RECORDS

The level of accounting carried out will depend on the nature and size of the NGO, but the records kept usually include the following:

## CASH AND BANK BOOK (THE CASH BOOK)

A **cash and bank book** is kept by all organisations. It is likely to be either one or more physical books or listings, even if the information is subsequently transferred to a computerised system.

The cash and bank book records all money coming in and going out. The cash part of the book records cash items, and the bank part of the book records transactions through the bank account. Cash and bank transactions in the same currency can be recorded together on the same page of the cash book (Figure 5).

Amounts coming in, **receipts**, are usually listed on the left page of the book and amounts going out, **payments**, on the right.

The book containing cash and bank transactions either together or separately is often referred to, rather confusingly, as the **cash book**.

In most countries, ready lined cash books are available from large stationery shops. An alternative is to draw the columns shown in Figure 5 in an exercise book.

## KEY POINTS FROM THE CASH BOOK EXAMPLE

- In this example **opening balance** is used at the beginning and **closing balance** at the end of the month. The abbreviations **b/d** and **c/d** meaning the balance **brought down** and **carried down**, can be used to show totals at the beginning and end of an accounting period. **B/f** and **c/f** meaning the balance **brought forward** and **carried forward** are used at the beginning and end of a page.
- The total figures at the bottom of the two cash columns (14,515.06) must agree, as must the figures at the bottom of the two bank columns (181,896.74).
- The closing cash balance of 2,910.59 included above the total means that the two cash columns agree. The cash closing balance will be represented by the physical amount of cash actually held at the end of the month. The physical cash should be counted at the month's end *to ensure it is the same as* the cash closing balance figure.

  The bank closing balance (78,460.07) will be the Lomtaka Centre's own record of the amount it has in the bank. This *must be agreed* with the closing balance that the bank shows on its **bank statement** (or **bank pass book**), although initially these two figures may be different. The bank reconciliation example on pages 41 and 42 shows how to agree these two figures.

**CASH BOOK FOR THE LOMTAKA RURAL HEALTH CARE CENTRE: 1–31 JANUARY (YEAR 2)**

**RECEIPTS**

| Date | Details | Receipt number | Cash | Bank |
|---|---|---|---|---|
| 1 Jan | Opening balance | - | 4,780.78 | 25,604.56 |
| 4 Jan | Fees and charges 1-4 Jan | R1 | 150.00 | |
| 6 Jan | Fees and charges 5-6 Jan | R2 | 357.23 | |
| 7 Jan | Donation | R3 | 294.39 | |
| 7 Jan | Fees and charges | R4 | 173.10 | |
| 9 Jan | Department of Health | R5 | | 150,000.00 |
| 9 Jan | Fees and charges 8-9 Jan | R6 | 460.22 | |
| 10 Jan | Cash to bank | - | | 2,992.84 |
| 10 Jan | Cashed cheque | - | 5,000.00 | |
| 13 Jan | Fees and charges 10-13 Jan | R7 | 150.29 | |
| 14 Jan | Fees and charges | R8 | 421.71 | |
| 15 Jan | Donation | R9 | 20.00 | |
| 15 Jan | Fees and charges | R10 | 189.34 | |
| 18 Jan | Fees and charges 16-18 Jan | R11 | 427.13 | |
| 23 Jan | Fees and charges 19-23 Jan | R12 | 385.08 | |
| 28 Jan | Fees and charges 24-28 Jan | R13 | 1,386.59 | |
| 31 Jan | Fees and charges 29-31 Jan | R14 | 319.20 | |
| 31 Jan | Cash to bank | - | | 3,299.34 |
| | | | 14,515.06 | 181,896.74 |

**PAYMENTS**

| Date | Details | Payment number | Cheque number | Cash | Bank |
|---|---|---|---|---|---|
| 1 Jan | Rent: T. Chibaya | P1 | 374623 | | 10,000.00 |
| 4 Jan | Petrol | P2 | | 500.00 | |
| 6 Jan | Travel expenses | P3 | | 189.38 | |
| 6 Jan | Medical supplies | P4 | | 2,023.00 | |
| 6 Jan | Photocopies | P5 | | 31.50 | |
| 7 Jan | Medical supplies | P6 | | 250.07 | |
| 9 Jan | Drugs | P7 | 374624 | | 35,896.38 |
| 10 Jan | Cash to bank | - | | 2,992.84 | |
| 10 Jan | Cashed cheque | - | 374625 | | 5,000.00 |
| 13 Jan | Advance: AG | P8 | | 1,000.00 | |
| 14 Jan | Telephone invoice | P9 | 374626 | | 839.00 |
| 18 Jan | Travel | P10 | | 237.10 | |
| 18 Jan | Vehicle repairs | P11 | 374627 | | 1,092.50 |
| 21 Jan | Photocopies | P12 | | 25.95 | |
| 22 Jan | Training fees | P13 | 374628 | | 602.37 |
| 22 Jan | Photocopies | P15 | | 55.29 | |
| 25 Jan | Medical supplies | P16 | 374629 | | 5,089.47 |
| 26 Jan | Travel advance: AG | P17 | | 1,000.00 | |
| 31 Jan | Salaries | P18 | 374630 | | 44,916.95 |
| 31 Jan | Cash to bank | - | | 3,299.34 | |
| | *Total payments* | | | 11,604.47 | 103,436.67 |
| 31 Jan | Closing balance | | | 2,910.59 | 78,460.07 |
| | | | | 14,515.06 | 181,896.74 |

**Figure 5: Cash book for the Lomtaka Centre showing receipts and payments for January (year 2)**

- When the cheque for 5,000.00 is cashed (10 January), both the bank and the cash parts of the cash book are affected. The payments side of the bank part shows the transaction as an amount going *out*, and the receipts side of the cash part as an amount coming in. Overall, no money has been spent, only transferred from bank to cash!
- Similarly, when cash is paid into the bank (for example 2,992.84 on 10 January), bank receipts increase and cash is reduced.
- Some amounts received will be paid directly into the bank account, for example the Department of Health grant of 150,000.00 (9 January). When the confirmation from the bank for its arrival has been received, this entry should be included in the bank receipts section of the organisation's cash and bank book.
- **Receipts** are the signed pieces of paper used to acknowledge money that has been received or paid, and must be kept for all transactions. (The word 'receipts' means two things in accounting language – money coming in *and* the signed pieces of paper.)

  Receipts (or **vouchers**) must be kept for money received in one file, and for money paid out in another. A separate sequence of numbers should be kept for each. In this example the letter 'R' is used to indicate a receipt number, and 'P' to indicate a payment number. All documents supporting the transaction, for example receipts, **invoices**, requests for payment and letters, should be filed.

  Any receipt issued should be pre-numbered and clearly show the name of the organisation. This ensures that only official receipts are used.
- Cheque numbers are shown in a column on the payments side.
- To provide details of the budget category of receipts and payments, an extra column might be added on each side of the book to include a written description of the transaction, for example 'salaries'. A series of account codes may be included to make this easier. The Lomtaka Centre might code its expenditure as follows.

| | | |
|---|---|---|
| S = salaries | R = rent | D = purchase of drugs |
| M = medical supplies | E = electricity | TE = travelling expenses |
| TP = training programme | OC = office costs (including audit) | |

Alternatively, a numerical account code can be used, especially if the data is, or will subsequently be, input to a computer. A summary of the items included in these codes could then be produced at the end of each month. An **analysed cash book** (see below) makes this process a lot easier.

Most NGOs will benefit from developing account codes to suit their own needs, rather than just using a standard list. This set of account codes is

often described as a **chart of accounts**. It may be necessary to consult a qualified accountant to help design such a system.
• The cash book should be written up and paperwork numbered and filed each time a transaction takes place.

## MORE THAN ONE CURRENCY

When transactions are in more than one currency, a separate cash book or separate parts of the same book must be maintained for each currency.

Transfers between currencies must be reflected in each currency's cash book. *Both entries should show the corresponding amount in the other currency as information, in the details column of the cash book.* Any paperwork relating to transfers between currencies must always be kept.

**Examples:**

• If $1,000.00 from the US$ bank account is transferred into Sh.62,000.00 in the Kenyan Shillings bank account, the entries in the cash books will be as follows.

$1,000.00 will be shown on the payments side of the US$ bank account record and Sh. 62,000.00 on the receipts side of the Kenyan Shillings bank account record.

• If $250 from the US$ cash account is transferred into the Kenya Shillings bank account, becoming an amount of Sh.15,500.00, the entries will be as follows.

$250.00 will be shown on the payments side of the US$ cash account record and Sh.15,500.00 shown on the receipts side of the Kenyan Shillings bank account record.

## ANALYSED CASH BOOK FOR THE LOMTAKA RURAL HEALTH CARE CENTRE: 1–31 JANUARY (YEAR 2)

### RECEIPTS SIDE

| Date | Details | Receipt number | Cash | Bank | WEV Grant | Donoraid Grant | Dept. of Health | Fees and Charges | Other Receipts |
|---|---|---|---|---|---|---|---|---|---|
| 1 Jan | Opening balance | - | 4,780.78 | 25,604.56 | | | | | 30,385.34 |
| 4 Jan | Fees and charges 1-4 Jan | R1 | 150.00 | | | | | 150.00 | |
| 6 Jan | Fees and charges 5-6 Jan | R2 | 357.23 | | | | | 357.23 | |
| 7 Jan | Donation | R3 | 294.39 | | | | | | 294.39 |
| 7 Jan | Fees and charges | R4 | 173.10 | | | | | 173.10 | |
| 9 Jan | Department of Health | R5 | | 150,000.00 | | | 150,000.00 | | |
| 9 Jan | Fees and charges 8-9 Jan | R6 | 460.22 | | | | | 460.22 | |
| 10 Jan | Cash to bank | - | | 2,992.84 | | | | | 2,992.84 |
| 10 Jan | Cashed cheque | - | 5,000.00 | | | | | | 5,000.00 |
| 13 Jan | Fees and charges 10-13 Jan | R7 | 150.29 | | | | | 150.29 | |
| 14 Jan | Fees and charges | R8 | 421.71 | | | | | 421.71 | |
| 15 Jan | Donation | R9 | 20.00 | | | | | | 20.00 |
| 15 Jan | Fees and charges | R10 | 189.34 | | | | | 189.34 | |
| 18 Jan | Fees and charges 16-18 Jan | R11 | 427.13 | | | | | 427.13 | |
| 23 Jan | Fees and charges 19-23 Jan | R12 | 385.08 | | | | | 385.08 | |
| 28 Jan | Fees and charges 24-28 Jan | R13 | 1,386.59 | | | | | 1,386.59 | |
| 31 Jan | Fees and charges 29-31 Jan | R14 | 319.20 | | | | | 319.20 | |
| 31 Jan | Cash to bank | - | | 3,299.34 | | | | | 3,299.34 |
| | | | 14,515.06 | 181,896.74 | - | - | 150,000.00 | 4,419.89 | 41,991.91 |

Figure 6: Analysed cash book for the Lomtaka Centre, receipts side only for January (year 2)

## ANALYSED CASH BOOK FOR THE LOMTAKA RURAL HEALTH CARE CENTRE: 1–31 JANUARY (YEAR 2)

### PAYMENTS SIDE

| Date | Details | Payment number | Cheque number | Cash | Bank | Salaries | Rent of Premises | Purchase of Drugs | Medical Supplies | Electricity | Travelling expenses | Training programme | Office Costs | Other Payments |
|---|---|---|---|---|---|---|---|---|---|---|---|---|---|---|
| 1 Jan | Rent: T. Chibaya | P1 | 374623 | | 10,000.00 | | 10,000.00 | | | | | | | |
| 4 Jan | Petrol | P2 | | 500.00 | | | | | | | 500.00 | | | |
| 6 Jan | Travel expenses | P3 | | 189.38 | | | | | | | 189.38 | | | |
| 6 Jan | Medical supplies | P4 | | 2,023.00 | | | | | 2,023.00 | | | | | |
| 6 Jan | Photocopies | P5 | | 31.50 | | | | | | | | | 31.50 | |
| 7 Jan | Medical supplies | P6 | | 250.07 | | | | | 250.07 | | | | | |
| 9 Jan | Drugs | P7 | 374624 | | 35,896.38 | | | 35,896.38 | | | | | | |
| 10 Jan | Cash to bank | - | | 2,992.84 | | | | | | | | | | 2,992.84 |
| 10 Jan | Cashed cheque | - | 374625 | | 5,000.00 | | | | | | | | | 5,000.00 |
| 13 Jan | Advance: AG | P8 | | 1,000.00 | | | | | | | | | | 1,000.00 |
| 14 Jan | Telephone invoice | P9 | 374626 | | 839.00 | | | | | | | | 839.00 | |
| 18 Jan | Travel | P10 | | 237.10 | | | | | | | 237.10 | | | |
| 18 Jan | Vehicle repairs | P11 | 374627 | | 1,092.50 | | | | | | 1,092.50 | | | |
| 21 Jan | Photocopies | P12 | | 25.95 | | | | | | | | | 25.95 | |
| 22 Jan | Training fees | P13 | 374628 | | 602.37 | | | | | | | 602.37 | | |
| 22 Jan | Photocopies | P15 | | 55.29 | | | | | | | | | 55.29 | |
| 25 Jan | Medical supplies | P16 | 374629 | | 5,089.47 | | | | 5,089.47 | | | | | |
| 26 Jan | Travel advance: AG | P17 | | 1,000.00 | | | | | | | | | | 1,000.00 |
| 31 Jan | Salaries | P18 | 374630 | | 44,916.95 | 44,916.95 | | | | | | | | |
| 31 Jan | Cash to bank | - | | 3,299.34 | | | | | | | | | | 3,299.34 |
| | *Total payments* | | | 11,604.47 | 103,436.67 | 44,916.95 | 10,000.00 | 35,896.38 | 7,362.54 | - | 2,018.98 | 602.37 | 951.74 | 81,370.66 |
| 31 Jan | Closing balance | | | 2,910.59 | 78,460.07 | | | | | | | | | |
| | | | | 14,515.06 | 181,896.74 | 44,916.95 | 10,000.00 | 35,896.38 | 7,362.54 | - | 2,018.98 | 602.37 | 951.74 | 94,662.84 |

**Figure 7: Analysed cash book for the Lomtaka Centre, payments side only for January (year 2)**

## ANALYSED CASH BOOK

A variation on the cash book is the **analysed cash book**, which allows more analysis of the types of receipt and payment. This replaces the basic cash book – it is not necessary to keep both.

The extra column headings in the analysed cash book include the same titles as those in the budget. Therefore, in addition to the daily recording of amounts coming in to and going out of the cash and bank accounts, the analysed cash book has extra columns to record to which budget item the transaction belongs. Figures 6 and 7 show the Lomtaka Centre's analysed cash book for the month of January (year 2). Here it is shown on two pages, as it is too wide to fit on one page.

## KEY POINTS FROM THE ANALYSED CASH BOOK EXAMPLE

- At 31 January, the totals at the bottom of the analysed part of the *receipts* side of the book (150,000.00 + 4,419.89 + 41,991.91 = **196,411.80**), will total the same as the cash and bank columns added together (14,515.06 + 181,896.74 = **196,411.80**).
- The totals of the columns at 31 January on the *payments* side (44,916.95 + 10,000.00 + 35,896.38 + 7,362.54 + 2,018.98 + 602.37 + 951.74 + 94,662.84 = **196,411.80**) are the same as the cash and bank columns (14,515.06 + 181,896.74 = **196,411.80**).
- The headings in the receipts and payments analysis columns, should follow the headings in the budget. The amounts at the end of the month can then be compared with the budget. The budgeted amounts for the year may in fact be written at the top of each column as a guide.
- The two columns 'other receipts' and 'other payments' include those items not in the budget, for example, opening and closing balances, transfers between cash and bank and unaccounted for advances.
- The analysed cash book can provide the data for updating the month of January in the cash budget (see Chapter 2). If this is done, figures for cashed cheques and the opening and closing balances from the analysed cash book would be excluded.
- Analysed cash books can be drawn up by hand, but in most countries pre-printed books are available from large stationery shops. A column should be included for each part of the budget, with further columns if a breakdown is required of a particular item. Allow as much room as possible. As in this example, more columns are usually required for the payments side than the receipts side.

- The analysed cash book can also be completed using a computer spreadsheet package.

## ADVANCES REGISTER

'Advances' in the analysed cash book payments in Figure 7 are cash amounts given to an employee for use on expenses relating to the person's work – *not* as a salary advance. The two advances, 1,000.00 (13 January) and 1,000.00 (26 January) to 'AG' have been analysed as 'other payments' even though one of these is for 'travel' (26 January). It will not be known what either advance has been spent on until it is accounted for by 'AG' at a later date. The advances are therefore included in the 'other payments' columns to prevent them being unaccounted for.

A *separate record* – **the advances register** – should be kept to record advances given and accounts received. This is in addition to the entry in the cash or analysed cash book. A suggested format is shown in Figure 8. Someone must be responsible for this to ensure that all advances are fully accounted for by the individual who received the money (this needs to be enforced by someone with a strong personality!).

| Date | Name | Advance Amount | Signature | Reason | Balance returned Date    Amount | Date accounts submitted | Officer actioning |
|------|------|----------------|-----------|--------|--------------------------------|-------------------------|-------------------|
| 13.1 | AG   | 1,000.00       | A. G...... | Travel | -          -                    | 17.1  1,000.00          | A Cashier         |
| 26.1 | AG   | 1,000.00       | A. G...... | Travel |                                |                         |                   |

**Figure 8: Layout of the Lomtaka Centre's advances register**

The advances register should be reviewed regularly to make sure that amounts have not built up without being accounted for. Staff who have not presented their accounts after one month, need to be asked to produce them.

When accounts are received and all the advance is accounted for, an amount is transferred in the analysed cash book out of the 'other payments' column into the appropriate column(s) for the expenditure. The analysed cash book example shows that 'AG' had been given the advance on 13 January. If, on 17 January, 1,000.00 was accounted for with appropriate receipts to show the advance had been spent as 850.00 on travel and 150.00 on office costs, the alteration in the analysed cash book would have been as follows.

| Date | Details | Payment number | Cheque number | Cash | Bank | Travelling Expenses | Training Programme | Office Costs | Other Payments |
|------|---------|------|------|------|------|------|------|------|------|
| 1 Jan | Rent: T. Chibaya | P1 | 374623 | | 10,000.00 | | | | |
| 4 Jan | Petrol | P2 | | 500.00 | | 500.00 | | | |
| 6 Jan | Travel expenses | P3 | | 189.38 | | 189.38 | | | |
| 6 Jan | Medical supplies | P4 | | 2,023.00 | | | | | |
| 6 Jan | Photocopies | P5 | | 31.50 | | | | 31.50 | |
| 7 Jan | Medical supplies | P6 | | 250.07 | | | | | |
| 9 Jan | Drugs | P7 | 374624 | | 35,896.38 | | | | |
| 10 Jan | Cash to bank | - | | 2,992.84 | | | | | 2,992.84 |
| 10 Jan | Cashed cheque | - | 374625 | | 5,000.00 | | | | 5,000.00 |
| **13 Jan** | **Advance: AG** | **P8** | | **1,000.00** | | | | | **1,000.00** |
| 14 Jan | Telephone invoice | P9 | 374626 | | 839.00 | | | 839.00 | |
| **17 Jan** | **AG advance returned** | **P10** | | | | **850.00** | | **150.00** | **(1,000.00)** |

**Figure 9: Effect of advances on the Lomtaka Centre's analysed cash book**

The only effect of this would be to correct the analysis columns. No alterations would be necessary in the bank and cash columns. This transfer could happen in a subsequent month.

If the money is not really an advance but for something specific, it should be described as such by the original entry in the cash book and an invoice obtained.

## PETTY CASH

The format of the **petty cash** book can be the same as the cash book example in Figure 5 but without the bank columns. A cash book or analysed cash book layout can be used to record the items. Receipts (the pieces of paper) for the money coming in and going out are essential and must be retained and filed.

The petty cash would normally be for a fixed amount of money – which is sometimes referred to as a **float**. The total of the receipts (the pieces of paper) for payments made and the remaining cash, should at any time be equal to the amount of the float. The remaining cash should be counted regularly by the cashier and agreed with the petty cash book. A senior member of staff should check the amount of cash agrees with the petty cash records on a regular basis.

When more money is needed in petty cash, cash or a cash cheque is issued from the main cash book, as a 'top-up' for the total of the receipts for items bought. This is shown as a payment in the main cash book and a receipt in the petty cash book.

A small organisation might refer to the main cash book as 'petty cash'. A large organisation, especially one based on several sites, might hold a number of petty cash accounts, in addition to the central main cash book. A petty cash book should be kept by someone other than the person responsible for the main cash book, to make the system more secure.

# BANK ACCOUNTS AND BANK RECONCILIATION

## BANK ACCOUNTS

Most NGOs should open a bank account, unless their geographical location makes this impossible. Banks are likely to offer a number of options, including a

- **current account**
  Cheques can be drawn on this account and amounts paid in.
- **deposit account**
  An account that gains interest. Surplus funds may be temporarily placed in this account. There may be a period of notice (for example, 7 days) before deposited money can be withdrawn.

For all accounts, a record of transactions in and out should be held in the bank part of the cash book. The bank will regularly send a **bank statement** or update a **bank pass book** to show the transactions which it has recorded. A **bank reconciliation** (see below) should be prepared to confirm that the NGO's and bank's records agree.

Some large donors require a separate bank account for their funds. This is often unnecessary if the financial records show clear accounting information about the grants received and full details on how they have been spent.

## BANK RECONCILIATION

A bank reconciliation should be prepared whenever a bank statement is received (or a bank pass book is updated). It involves identifying the reasons for any difference between the organisation's cash book balance and the bank statement balance at a particular date.

Reasons for a difference are likely to be:

- the NGO's cheques have been written and entered into the bank part of its cash

book but have not yet been presented by the recipients, through their bank;
- amounts paid into the bank by the organisation have not yet been credited on the bank statement;
- items on the bank statement, which are not yet in the NGO's cash book. For example, **bank charges**, **bank interest** and items received or paid by the bank on the organisation's behalf;
- errors in the NGO's cash book, or on the bank statement or pass book.

A bank reconciliation example is completed on pages 41 and 42, using the Lomtaka Centre's cash/bank book, and its bank statement from the National Bank of Commerce. The steps taken to achieve this are shown in Figure 10.

---

### 5 STEPS TO COMPLETE A BANK RECONCILIATION

1. Ensure that the balance in the *cash book and the balance in the bank statement at the beginning of the period agree*. If not, you need to know the reason for this. If there was a bank reconciliation at the end of the previous period, this should explain any difference.

2. *The cash book is updated* to the end of the month, as far as possible.

3. *Items* appearing in the bank columns of the cash book *and* on the bank statement *are ticked off*.

4. *A bank reconciliation statement is prepared* using the items not ticked.

5. The *figures* from the cash book and the bank statement *should then agree*.

---

**Figure 10: Steps to be taken in completing a bank reconciliation**

Bank charges of 348.00 are included on the Lomtaka Centre's bank statement (31 January) but not in the bank part of their cash book. The Centre was not aware of these until after the cash book had been completed and the bank statement received.

The charges need to be included in the bank column of the cash book. By including the charges in the bank column of the February cash book (which is probably when the statement was received), the reconciliation shows the difference at the end of January.

Payments made by the bank on the NGO's behalf should be treated in the same way when they appear on the bank statement.

## BANK RECONCILIATION EXAMPLE

**<u>Page 1 of the example</u>** shows the cash book. Items appearing in both the cash book and bank statement have been ticked off.

**<u>Page 2 of the example</u>** shows the bank statement. Items appearing in both the cash book and bank statement have been ticked off. It also shows how the bank reconciliation statement itself can be presented.

**BANK RECONCILIATION EXAMPLE (page 1)**

**CASH BOOK FOR THE LOMTAKA HEALTH CARE CENTRE: 1–31 JANUARY (YEAR 2)**

### RECEIPTS

| Date | Details | Rec. no. | Cash | Bank | |
|---|---|---|---|---|---|
| 1 Jan | Opening balance | - | 4,780.78 | 25,604.56 | |
| 4 Jan | Fees and charges 1-4 Jan | R1 | 150.00 | | |
| 6 Jan | Fees and charges 5-6 Jan | R2 | 357.23 | | |
| 7 Jan | Donation | R3 | 294.39 | | |
| 7 Jan | Fees and charge | R4 | 173.10 | | ✓ |
| 9 Jan | Department of Health | R5 | | 150,000.00 | |
| 9 Jan | Fees and charges 8-9 Jan | R6 | 460.22 | | ✓ |
| 10 Jan | Cash to bank | - | | 2,992.84 | |
| 10 Jan | Cashed cheque | - | 5,000.00 | | |
| 13 Jan | Fees and charges 10-13 Jan | R7 | 150.29 | | |
| 14 Jan | Fees and charges | R8 | 421.71 | | |
| 15 Jan | Donation | R9 | 20.00 | | |
| 15 Jan | Fees and charges | R10 | 189.34 | | |
| 18 Jan | Fees and charges 16-18 Jan | R11 | 427.13 | | |
| 23 Jan | Fees and charges 19-23 Jan | R12 | 385.08 | | |
| 28 Jan | Fees and charges 24-28 Jan | R13 | 1,386.59 | | |
| 31 Jan | Fees and charges 29-31 Jan | R14 | 319.20 | | o/s |
| 31 Jan | Cash to bank | - | | 3,299.34 | |
| | | | 14,515.06 | 181,896.74 | |

### PAYMENTS

| Date | Details | Pay. no. | Cheque number | Cash | Bank | |
|---|---|---|---|---|---|---|
| 1 Jan | Rent: T. Chibaya | P1 | 374623 | | 10,000.00 | ✓ |
| 4 Jan | Petrol | P2 | | 500.00 | | |
| 6 Jan | Travel expenses | P3 | | 189.38 | | |
| 6 Jan | Medical supplies | P4 | | 2,023.00 | | |
| 6 Jan | Photocopies | P5 | | 31.50 | | |
| 7 Jan | Medical supplies | P6 | | 250.07 | | |
| 9 Jan | Drugs | P7 | 374624 | | 35,896.38 | ✓ |
| 10 Jan | Cash to bank | - | | 2,992.84 | | ✓ |
| 10 Jan | Cashed cheque | - | 374625 | 1,000.00 | 5,000.00 | ✓ |
| 13 Jan | Advance: AG | P8 | | 1,000.00 | | |
| 14 Jan | Telephone invoice | P9 | 374626 | | 839.00 | o/s |
| 18 Jan | Travel | P10 | | 237.10 | | |
| 18 Jan | Vehicle repairs | P11 | 374627 | | 1,092.50 | o/s |
| 21 Jan | Photocopies | P12 | | 25.95 | | |
| 22 Jan | Training fees | P13 | 374628 | | 602.37 | ✓ |
| 22 Jan | Photocopies | P15 | | 55.29 | | |
| 25 Jan | Medical supplies | P16 | 374629 | | 5,089.47 | ✓ |
| 26 Jan | Travel advance: AG | P17 | | 1,000.00 | | |
| 31 Jan | Salaries | P18 | 374630 | | 44,916.95 | |
| 31 Jan | Cash to bank | - | | 3,299.34 | | |
| | Total payments | | | 11,604.47 | 103,436.67 | |
| 31 Jan | Closing balance | | | 2,910.59 | 78,460.07 | |
| | | | | 14,515.06 | 181,896.74 | |

## BANK RECONCILIATION EXAMPLE (page 2)

### NATIONAL BANK OF COMMERCE

### ACCOUNT: LOMTAKA HEALTH CARE CENTRE

Statement for the period: 1–31 January

| Date | Details | Debit | Credit | Balance |
|---|---|---|---|---|
| 1 Jan | Balance b/forward **Re** | | | 23,780.49 |
| 1 Jan | Credit **December** | | 2,218.20 | 25,998.69 |
| 4 Jan | Cheque 374621 | 394.13 | | 25,604.56 |
| 4 Jan | Cheque 374623 | 10,000.00 ✓ | | 15,604.56 |
| 9 Jan | Transfer | | 150,000.00 ✓ | 165,604.56 |
| 10 Jan | Credit | | 2,992.84 ✓ | 168,597.40 |
| 10 Jan | Cheque 374625 | 5,000.00 ✓ | | 163,597.40 |
| 13 Jan | Cheque 374624 | 35,896.38 ✓ | | 127,701.02 |
| 18 Jan | Cheque 374626 | 839.00 ✓ | | 126,862.02 |
| 29 Jan | Cheque 374629 | 5,089.47 ✓ | | 121,772.55 |
| 31 Jan | Cheque 374630 | 44,916.95 ✓ | | 76,855.60 |
| 31 Jan | Charges | 348.00 **O/S** | | 76,507.60 |
| 31 Jan | Balance c/forward | | | 76,507.60 |

o/s  =  outstanding

### BANK RECONCILIATION STATEMENT

Balance as shown in the bank statement at 31 January (year 2)  **76,507.60**

*DEDUCT* CHEQUES NOT YET PRESENTED

| Date | Cheque number | Amount |
|---|---|---|
| 18 Jan | 374627 | 1,092.50 |
| 22 Jan | 374628 | 602.37 |

**TOTAL TO DEDUCT**  **(1,694.87)**

*ADD* AMOUNTS PAID IN, NOT YET CREDITED

| Date | Reference | Amount |
|---|---|---|
| 31 Jan | Cash to bank | 3,299.34 |

**TOTAL TO ADD**  **3,299.34**

*OTHER ADJUSTMENTS*

| | | |
|---|---|---|
| Bank charges | 348.00 | **348.00** |

**Balance in cash book at 31 January (year 2)**  **78,460.07**

## KEY POINTS FROM THE BANK RECONCILIATION EXAMPLE

- The reconciliation shows why the closing balance on the bank part of the cash book and that of the bank statement, do not agree.
- The two items at the start of the bank statement (credit 2,218.20 on 1 January and cheque 374621 for 394.13 on 4 January) relate to the previous month. These items do not appear in the bank part of the January cash book at all, and it can be seen that the cheque number for the second item was in the sequence used before the start of the January cash book.

  This credit for 2,218.20 and cheque 374621 for 394.13 can be ignored as they have now appeared on the statement. In fact, the balance after they have been included on the bank statement is 25,604.56, which is the opening bank balance on 1 January in the cash book. The December (year 1) bank reconciliation statement would have shown these items as outstanding. If one of these items had *not* appeared on the January bank statement, it would also be included in the end of January bank reconciliation.
- Cheques 374627 (1,092.50) and 374628 (602.37) and the amount paid into the bank on 31 January (3,299.34) are still outstanding, but can be expected to appear on the bank statement in February.
- The figure for bank charges has been included in the bank reconciliation statement as the details were received on the bank statement (received in February). It will therefore be included in the bank part of the February cash book.

# RECEIPTS AND PAYMENTS ACCOUNT

A **receipts and payments account** is a summary of all cash and bank items coming in to and going out of an NGO and is usually prepared at the end of the financial year. It is the simplest form of accounting statement. It includes different types of receipt and payment together. The purchase of items to be used in the long term, for example vehicles and computers, are listed alongside all the day-to-day items such as rent, salaries or grants. **Loans** and **capital grants** are also included.

The data needed to prepare a receipts and payments account comes primarily from the cash (and bank) book. The account shows the amount held in cash and at the bank at the beginning and end of the period. The receipts and payments account does *not* however show whether a **surplus** or a **deficit** has been made, and for this reason is of limited use as a comparison with the budget.

The receipts and payments account is usually produced by small groups, with a single purpose or activity, and with few staff. However, some NGOs with more complex operations use the account because of its simplicity.

Its main advantage is that the cash book can usually be maintained and the receipts and payments account prepared by someone who is not trained in the technical aspects of accounting.

There are a number of ways in which the receipts and payments account can be presented. Two formats are shown below, with the same information included in each example. A further format is shown in Example 1 of Appendix C.

---

**LOMTAKA HEALTH CARE CENTRE**
**RECEIPTS AND PAYMENTS ACCOUNT FOR THE YEAR ENDED**
**31 DECEMBER (YEAR 1)**

| RECEIPTS | | PAYMENTS | |
|---|---|---|---|
| Cash/bank balance at 1 January | 0* | Salaries | 483,109 |
| Grants   - WEV | 100,000 | Rent of premises | 96,000 |
|    - Donoraid | 240,000 | Purchase of drugs | 95,900 |
| Department of Health | 350,000 | Medical supplies | 56,794 |
| Fees and charges | 90,974 | Electricity | 11,547 |
| Other income | 20,023 | Travelling expenses | 18,394 |
| Department of Health | 45,000 | Training programme | 5,293 |
| (capital grant) | | Office costs (including audit) | 10,887 |
| Bank loan | 10,000 | Other payments | 2,192 |
| | | Purchase of vehicle | 15,298 |
| | | Purchase of equipment | 30,198 |
| | | Cash/bank balance at | |
| | | 31 December | 30,385 |
| | **855,997** | | **855,997** |

---

\* No opening cash and bank balance is included because this is the first year of operation.

**LOMTAKA HEALTH CARE CENTRE**
**RECEIPTS AND PAYMENTS ACCOUNT FOR THE YEAR ENDED**
**31 DECEMBER (YEAR 1)**

| | | |
|---|---:|---:|
| **Cash and bank balance at 1 January** | | **0\*** |
| | | |
| **RECEIPTS** | | |
| Grants - WEV | 100,000 | |
|        - Donoraid | 240,000 | |
| Department of Health | 350,000 | |
| Fees and charges | 90,974 | |
| Other income | 20,023 | |
| Department of Health (capital grant) | 45,000 | |
| Bank loan | 10,000 | 855,997 |
| | | 855,997 |
| | | |
| **PAYMENTS** | | |
| Salaries | 483,109 | |
| Rent of premises | 96,000 | |
| Purchase of drugs | 95,900 | |
| Medical supplies | 56,794 | |
| Electricity | 11,547 | |
| Travelling expenses | 18,394 | |
| Training programme | 5,293 | |
| Office costs (including audit) | 10,887 | |
| Other payments | 2,192 | |
| Purchase of vehicle | 15,298 | |
| Purchase of equipment | 30,198 | 825,612 |
| **Cash and bank balance at 31 December** | | **30,385** |

\* No opening cash and bank balance is included because this is the first year of operation.

**Figure 11: Two presentations of a receipts and payments account**

## KEY POINTS FROM THE RECEIPTS AND PAYMENTS ACCOUNT

- Both formats are widely used. The second presentation shows two columns. The reason for this is to produce a sub-total for each of the *receipts* and *payments* figures.
- All items whether revenue or capital items are included together.

- The figures included are merely a record of what *has been received or paid during the year*. No adjustments have been made.
- In the example shown, only 240,000.00 is received from Donoraid. The figure of 250,000.00 was expected and listed in the budget (page 1 of the Budget Planning Example in Chapter 1). The additional 10,000.00 may in fact have been received in the following financial year in which case it would be included in the following year's account. This makes comparisons with the budget very difficult!

## IMPROVEMENTS TO THE RECEIPTS AND PAYMENTS ACCOUNT

There are a number of ways of improving the presentation to give more information. This is by adding notes to the account to show:

- A breakdown of any unclear items, in this example this might be *other income* and *other payments*.
- A list of outstanding amounts – **creditors** (money owed to other people by the organisation), and **debtors** (money that other people owe to the organisation). An example of a debtor would be the 10,000.00 outstanding from Donoraid, mentioned in the 'Key Points' above.
- Details of amounts not included in the account. For example, if the rent figure of 96,000.00 were to include only eleven months rent (actually, here it is the full twelve months!), it would be useful to say so in a note.
- Any items paid included in the figures shown, which actually relate to the following year.
- A list of long-term items owned, bought in previous years. Examples of these might be computers, equipment and vehicles. If the age of the item can also be included this helps to indicate when it will need to be replaced.
- Balances of any other cash or bank accounts held. They should all be included in the main receipts and payments account, but sometimes they are not! These additional accounts may include money put aside for the eventual replacement of long-term items such as vehicles.
- Repayment conditions relating to any loans.

A receipts and payments account is usually presented on its own. In some countries however the account is produced *together with* an **income and expenditure account** and **balance sheet** (these other statements are examined in Chapter 5).

# Chapter 4

## Further Records Kept to Produce More Detailed Accounting Data

---

**OBJECTIVES OF THIS CHAPTER**

This chapter examines the additional records kept in a 'double-entry book-keeping system'. Specimens of some of the records are shown but the technical aspects of double-entry are not described.

It is useful to have an overview of what is meant by double-entry book-keeping, but it is not necessary to understand the technicalities to be able to interpret accounting information. *If you find this chapter is getting too technical try and obtain a feel for the records kept and move on to Chapter 5.*

Having considered the material and specimen data in this chapter, you should be able to:

- summarise what is meant by double-entry book-keeping;
- describe the records kept when using this system;
- explain what is meant by a 'trial balance';
- outline the difference between the level of staff required to maintain basic accounting records and a double-entry book-keeping system.

---

The accounting records described in Chapter 3 are maintained by nearly all NGOs. None of these records necessitate technical accounting knowledge, and are relatively straightforward to maintain.

The additional records described in this chapter are kept where there is a **double-entry book-keeping** system. These are technically more difficult to maintain, and require someone with accounting training and experience. The benefit of double-entry is that it can provide more sophisticated management information.

# ACCOUNTING RECORDS NEEDED FOR DOUBLE-ENTRY BOOK-KEEPING

## THE LEDGER

The **ledger** divides money coming in or going out into types or classification known as an **account**, whereas the cash book divides money into *receipts* and *payments*. The ledger might include, for example, a travel account which would show all receipts and payments for travel. If the total amount spent on travel were needed, this figure would be readily available without adding up all the entries in the cash book. The ledger may either be a physical book or be kept as part of a computerised accounting system. An example from the Lomtaka Centre's ledger (year 2) is shown below.

| LEDGER | | | | | Page: 1 |
|---|---|---|---|---|---|
| Account name: | Rent paid account | | | Code: R | |
| | | | | | |
| **Date** | **Details** | **Ref.** | **Debit amount** | **Credit amount** | **Balance (Dr/Cr)** |
| 1 January | Bank:T. Chibaya Jan rent | CBJ1 | 10,000 | | 10,000dr |
| 1 February | "              Feb rent | CBF2 | 10,000 | | 20,000dr |
| 3 March | "              Mar rent | CBM1 | 10,000 | | 30,000dr |
| 31 March | "              Apr rent | CBM8 | 10,000 | | 40,000dr |
| 30 April | "              May rent | CBA7 | 10,000 | | 50,000dr |

**Figure 12: Extract of the rent account from the Lomtaka Centre's ledger**

Double-entry book-keeping dictates that every transaction has two entries in the ledger. If, for example, rent is paid by cheque, the ledger will record firstly that the amount of rent paid has increased and secondly that the bank account has decreased.

## Classification of accounts in the ledger

The ledger contains the following types of accounts.

| | |
|---|---|
| • **ASSETS** | Items *owned* by the organisation. For example, buildings, vehicles, stock, bank balance, cash accounts. |
| • **LIABILITIES** | Amounts *owed* by the organisation. For example, outstanding invoices from those who have provided goods and services (known as **creditors**) or **bank overdraft** accounts. |
| • **ACCUMULATED FUND/CAPITAL** | |
| | In *not-for-profit organisations* this is represented by previous years' surpluses (less any deficits) and any money raised or donated to start the organisation. This is often described as the **accumulated fund** or **reserves** account. |
| | In *commercial organisations* this is the amount invested in the business by its owner(s) and is referred to as the **capital** account. |
| • **EXPENSES** | Amounts paid *by* the organisation for its ongoing activities. For example salaries, rent, travelling expenses. |
| • **INCOME** | Amounts paid *to* the organisation. For example, grants, fees and charges accounts in not-for-profit organisations; the sales account in commercial organisations. |

**Figure 13: Categories of the accounts included in the ledger**

These classifications of accounts are the basis for the preparation of the financial statements shown in Chapter 5.

At the end of an accounting period, usually a financial year, a list of all the individual accounts will be put together in a **trial balance** (see below).

## THE JOURNAL

The **journal** is a permanent record of, for example, amendments to the ledger, the correction of errors and exchange rate adjustments. It is used only when a ledger is maintained, and enables anyone checking the accounts to see why the entries have been made and ensures they are properly authorised. The ledger itself will be adjusted in line with journal entries.

Cash or bank transactions usually have independent evidence – for example a receipt or an **invoice** – to verify the amount. For journal entries, there is no such evidence other than the entry in the journal itself. Each entry should therefore be *signed by someone in authority* to prove that the journal adjustment is genuine. The extra check can avert mistakes or potential fraud. Each entry in the journal has a description to say why it has been made.

| Voucher: 9 | **JOURNAL** | | | Page: 1 |
|---|---|---|---|---|
| **Date** | **Details** | **Reference** | **Debit amount** | **Credit amount** |
| 17 Feb | Office costs | OC | 58.00 | |
| " | Travel expenses | T | | 58.00 |
| | | | | |

Being an amount charged to AG's travel expenses (10 Feb) in error when it related to stationery purchased for the office.

**Authorised** ................................. **Date** ...................

**Figure 14: Example of the journal being used to correct an entry**

## TRIAL BALANCE

The **trial balance** is not actually one of 'the books of account'. It is a way of confirming the entries in the ledger are correct, prior to compiling further financial statements. It is prepared only when a ledger is maintained.

Two entries are made in the ledger for every transaction in terms of **debits** and **credits**.

- The *debit* balances are the asset and expense accounts.
- The *credit* balances are the liability, income and accumulated fund or capital accounts.

The trial balance lists the balance on each **account** (that is the individual account of the assets, liabilities, accumulated fund, expenses or income groups) in two columns, in terms of whether each one has a debit or a credit balance. The debit balances appear in the left column and the credit balances in the right column of the trial balance (see the Lomtaka example, Figure 15). If all entries have been made correctly, the trial balance columns agree – the total of all the debits equals the total of all the credits.

An example of the trial balance for the Lomtaka Centre at the end of year 1 is shown below. Some of the account names and amounts have already been used but some are additional ones. Two of these are: **debtors** – those who owe money to the Centre; and **creditors** – money that the Centre owes to other people.

| Lomtaka Health Care Centre: Trial Balance as at 31 December (year 1) | DEBIT | CREDIT |
|---|---|---|
| Grants   - WEV | | 100,000 |
| - Donoraid | | 240,000 |
| Department of Health | | 350,000 |
| Fees and charges | | 114,284 |
| Other income | | 20,023 |
| | | |
| Salaries | 483,109 | |
| Rent of premises | 96,000 | |
| Purchase of drugs | 104,621 | |
| Medical supplies | 61,309 | |
| Electricity | 11,547 | |
| Travelling expenses | 18,394 | |
| Training programme | 5,293 | |
| Office costs (including audit) | 10,887 | |
| Other payments | 2,192 | |
| | | |
| Vehicle (at cost) | 15,298 | |
| Equipment (at cost) | 30,198 | |
| Debtors | 23,310 | |
| Creditors | | 13,236 |
| Bank loan | | 10,000 |
| Bank/cash | 30,385 | |
| | | |
| Department of Health (capital grant) | | 45,000 |
| | **892,543** | **892,543** |

*The stock of drugs held at 31 December (year 1) is valued at 10,129.00.*

**Figure 15: The trial balance for the Lomtaka Centre (year 1)**

The trial balance provides the information needed to prepare the two main financial statements – the **balance sheet** and **income and expenditure account** (or in commercial organisations the **balance sheet** and **trading and profit and loss account**). These statements will be examined in Chapters 5, 6 and 7.

An NGO might have additional records to provide supporting data. These may include payroll records, a fixed assets register, and records for purchases and sales (of goods and services), if these are a large proportion of the activities.

*A full explanation of double-entry book-keeping is outside the scope of this book, but if you want to learn more there is a range of publications available on this subject.*

# APPOINTING FINANCIAL STAFF IN NGOs

Staff responsible for maintaining the financial records of an NGO must be trained and experienced. If the main record required is a cash/bank book, then a limited amount of technical accounting knowledge will be required. A practical test of whether a potential employee were competent to maintain this level of financial administration, would be if they could accurately prepare a bank reconciliation from data provided (a straightforward example of this is given in Chapter 3).

If the accounting system involves double-entry book-keeping and a ledger is maintained, it is essential to recruit a trained book-keeper. An indication of whether a potential employee has the appropriate skills would be if they could prepare an income and expenditure account including adjustments from a trial balance (an example of this is given in Chapter 6).

Larger NGOs or those with complex accounting needs might consider appointing a fully qualified **accountant**. This will be more expensive, but may be an appropriate 'investment' for the organisation. Evidence of the person's professional qualification and sound references is usually taken as a guide to their ability. An alternative to appointing a professionally qualified person may be to use the services of a local accounting firm.

If in doubt about appointing the appropriate level of staff, it is worthwhile consulting a qualified accountant. The benefits of financial staff with sound skills should never be underestimated.

# Chapter 5

## Income and Expenditure Account and Balance Sheet (First Drafts)

---

**OBJECTIVES OF THIS CHAPTER**

This chapter examines the differences between capital and revenue items. It introduces two main accounting statements – the income and expenditure account and the balance sheet.

Having considered the material and worked through the examples in this chapter, you should be able to:

- state the difference between revenue and capital income and expenditure;
- contrast the purposes of the income and expenditure account and the balance sheet;
- recognise a straightforward income and expenditure account and balance sheet;
- list some of the items which are included in each of the two statements;
- explain the difference between the income and expenditure account and the receipts and payment account.

---

## CAPITAL AND REVENUE

A classification which helps to separate items in the income and expenditure account from those in the balance sheet, is that of capital and revenue. These terms have already been used in Chapter 1.

**Capital expenditure** – expenditure on items which last for more than one year, for example, purchase of a vehicle, building or computer.

**Revenue expenditure** – expenditure on items which relate to one financial year only, for example, payment of salaries, rent or electricity.

Similarly, income can be separated into capital and revenue.

**Capital income** – money invested in an organisation for its long-term use, for example, capital grants or loans.

**Revenue income** – income received for an organisation's ongoing activities, for example, grants, fees and charges.

> - The *income and expenditure account* includes revenue income and revenue expenditure items.
> - The *balance sheet* includes capital income and capital expenditure items.

There are however some variations to the definition as many NGOs treat *capital expenditure* items that will last for more than one year but are of a relatively small value – perhaps under the equivalent of US$500.00 – as *revenue expenditure*. This is so that the accounting entries involved do not become too numerous.

It is however necessary to keep a list of all 'capital' items, whether above or below the specified amount, for security purposes. This list is often described as an **inventory**.

# FIRST DRAFT OF THE INCOME AND EXPENDITURE ACCOUNT

Chapter 3 considered the receipts and payments account, the simplest form of accounting statement. An alternative to this is the **income and expenditure account**, which is usually accompanied by a **balance sheet**. These two statements (or their equivalents) are usually produced when a double-entry system of accounting is in operation (see Chapter 4). The information in each statement is based on the trial balance summary of the ledger. An advantage of the income and expenditure account and the balance sheet, over the receipts and payments account, is that they are able to provide more sophisticated management information.

The data in the income and expenditure account, for example, is adjusted before it is produced, so it includes not only what has actually been received and paid, but also what *should* have been received and paid *for that financial year*. This means that a 'like-with-like' comparison can be made between the income and expenditure account and the budget.

The information contained in the following income and expenditure account for the Lomtaka Centre is based on the trial balance information for the Centre shown in Figure 15.

**Lomtaka Health Care Centre: Income and Expenditure account for the period ended 31 December (year 1) – FIRST DRAFT**

**Income**

| | | |
|---|---:|---:|
| Grants – WEV | | 100,000 |
| – Donoraid | | 240,000 |
| Department of Health | | 350,000 |
| Fees and charges | | 114,284 |
| Other income | | 20,023 |
| | | 824,307 |

**Expenditure**

| | | |
|---|---:|---:|
| Salaries | 483,109 | |
| Rent of premises | 96,000 | |
| Purchase of drugs | 104,621 | |
| Medical supplies | 61,309 | |
| Electricity | 11,547 | |
| Travelling expenses | 18,394 | |
| Training programme | 5,293 | |
| Office costs (including audit) | 10,887 | |
| Other payments | 2,192 | 793,352 |
| **Excess of income over expenditure** | | **30,955** |

Figure 16: The Lomtaka Centre's income and expenditure account (year 1) – first draft

## KEY POINTS FROM THE INCOME AND EXPENDITURE ACCOUNT

- Two columns of figures are included – this has nothing to do with debits and credits! It is merely a way of sub-totalling the expenditure figure (793,352.00).
- The income and expenditure account includes only *revenue* income and expenditure. *Capital* expenditure (the vehicle and equipment) and *capital* income (the capital grant and the bank loan) are placed in the balance sheet (see below).
- The **excess of income over expenditure** figure shows the **surplus** (the opposite of this, an **excess of expenditure over income**, would be described as a **deficit**).
- Further adjustments have still to be made to these figures, to include items such as **depreciation**. These adjustments will be shown in Chapter 6 .

## COMPARISON OF THE INCOME AND EXPENDITURE ACCOUNT WITH THE RECEIPTS AND PAYMENTS ACCOUNT

- The receipts and payments account shown in Chapter 3, Figure 11, records what has *actually* been received or paid. The income and expenditure account usually shows this plus what is *due* to be received or paid in the year, whether or not it has been! This enables a true comparison to be made with the budget.
- The income and expenditure account in Figure 16 records the total amounts that were *due* to have been received for fees and charges during the year (114,284.00). The difference between what has *actually* been received and the total *due* to have been received in this example, is described as **debtors** – those who owe the Lomtaka Centre money. The income and expenditure account includes the amount owed by debtors at the end of the year for fees and charges (in this case all the debtors!). This is *in addition to* the amount that has actually been received for fees and charges (shown in the receipts and payments account). This can be summarised as follows.

| | |
|---|---:|
| Fees and charges in the receipts and payments account *actually received* | 90,974 |
| + Amount of debtors for fees and charges outstanding at 31 December (year 1) | 23,310 |
| = Amount for fees and charges in the income and expenditure account | **114,284** |

- The amounts that *should* have been paid for purchase of drugs and medical supplies in addition to the amounts *actually* paid (shown in the receipts and payments account), are described as **creditors** – those to whom money is owed by the Centre. The income and expenditure account includes the creditors at the end of the year *in addition* to the amount actually received for purchase of drugs and medical supplies. This can be summarised as follows.

| | | |
|---|---:|---:|
| Purchase of drugs in the receipts and payments account *actually paid* | 95,900 | |
| Medical supplies in the receipts and payments account *actually paid* | 56,794 | 152,694 |
| + Amount of creditors outstanding at 31 December (year 1) (the creditors in this example relate to the purchase of drugs and to medical supplies) | | 13,236 |
| Purchase of drugs in the income and expenditure account | 104,621 | |
| Medical supplies in the income and expenditure account | 61,309 | **165,930** |

- The long-term items (capital grant from the Department of Health, bank loan and the purchase of vehicle and equipment) are included in the receipts and payments account but not in the income and expenditure account. The income and expenditure account contains only items that relate to the financial year in question – the 'running expenses' rather than items that relate to the long term. These long-term items are shown instead in the **balance sheet** (see below).

- The income and expenditure account does not show any cash or bank balances. These are included in the balance sheet (see below).

[NOTE: Legislation states that charities within the United Kingdom with a gross income of over £100,000 in sterling, are required to produce a Statement of Financial Activities in place of an Income and Expenditure account for their own UK accounting. This statement is outside the scope of this book.]

# FIRST DRAFT OF THE BALANCE SHEET

If an income and expenditure account (or its equivalent) is prepared, most NGOs will also produce a balance sheet.

The balance sheet produced at a particular point in time, usually the end of the financial year, shows what the organisation *owns* (its assets) and what it *owes* (its liabilities).

It divides assets and liabilities into short term (lasting up to a year) and long term (lasting more than a year). The balance sheet sections are shown below.

### The top part shows:
**Fixed assets:**  permanent items *owned* long term, for example buildings, vehicles and computers.

**Current assets:** items *owned* short term, for example stock, debtors (people who owe the organisation money) and the bank and cash balances.

*Less* **Current liabilities:** amounts *owed* and which will be paid in the short term, for example creditors (people to whom the organisation owes money) and bank overdrafts.

*Less* **Long-term liabilities:** amounts *owed* long term, for example bank loans of more than one year.

### The bottom part shows:
*The bottom part of the balance sheet (after 'financed by') records any long-*

term or 'capital' grants received, plus the cumulative total of previous years' surpluses (less any previous years' deficits) shown in each year's income and expenditure account. This might seem a mysterious figure! This is because the amount in the bottom part merely states where the money has come from (over however many years the organisation has been in existence) to finance what has happened in the top part. The total of the bottom part of the balance sheet must agree with the total of the top part.

In not-for-profit organisations, all of the bottom part of the balance sheet is often described as the:

**Accumulated fund:** items of long-term financing (for example capital grants received) plus previous years' surpluses (less any previous years' deficits).

The balance sheet can be presented in different ways, but the following format is common.

| Lomtaka Health Care Centre: Balance Sheet as at 31 December (year 1) FIRST DRAFT | | |
|---|---|---|
| **Fixed Assets** | | |
| Vehicle (at cost) | | 15,298 |
| Equipment (at cost) | | 30,198 |
| | | 45,496 |
| **Current Assets** | | |
| Debtors | 23,310 | |
| Bank and cash | 30,385 | |
| | 53,695 | |
| *Less:* **Current Liabilities** | | |
| Creditors | 13,236 | 40,459 |
| | | 85,955 |
| *Less:* **Long-term Liabilities** | | |
| Bank loan | | 10,000 |
| | | **75,955** |
| *Financed by:* | | |
| **Accumulated Fund** | | |
| Capital grant – Department of Health | | 45,000 |
| *Plus:* Excess of income over expenditure | | 30,955 |
| *(from the income and expenditure account)* | | |
| | | **75,955** |

**Figure 17: The Lomtaka Centre's balance sheet (year 1) – first draft**

## KEY POINTS FROM THE BALANCE SHEET

- The first column of figures is included to provide sub-totals for *current assets* and *current liabilities*.
- The figure 40,459.00 in the right hand column, is known as **working capital**.
- The purchase of vehicle and equipment, not shown in the income and expenditure account, is included in the balance sheet as part of the fixed assets.
- The accumulated fund represents the total of previous years' surpluses less previous years' deficits, together with any capital grants. As this is the first year of operation there is only the capital grant received *during* the year and the current year's surplus for the Lomtaka Centre.
- The accumulated fund at the start of year 2 will be 75,955.00. Any capital grants received in year 2 and any surplus will be added to this.
- Adjustments such as depreciation have not been made to the trial balance figures (see Chapter 6 for further adjustments).

The presentation of the balance sheet varies from country to country. Those similar to the above example start with the most permanent asset (land and buildings). Others start with the least permanent asset (cash) and progress to the fixed assets lower down the page. Examples of different presentations are shown in Appendix C.

Whatever the presentation or the terminology used, the following sections will be included in a balance sheet.

---

- **FIXED ASSETS**
- **CURRENT ASSETS**
- **CURRENT LIABILITIES**
- **LONG-TERM LIABILITIES**
- **ACCUMULATED FUND (ALSO CALLED CAPITAL, OR RESERVES)**

---

# Chapter 6

## Adjustments in Preparing the Final Accounting Statements

---

**OBJECTIVES OF THIS CHAPTER**

The aim of this chapter is to introduce adjustments to the trial balance in order to produce the final accounting statements (that is the income and expenditure and balance sheet). Try to get an understanding of why each of the adjustments has been made, and their impact on the first draft of the statements shown in Chapter 5, Figures 16 and 17.

Having considered the material and worked through the examples in this chapter, you should be able to:

- list the main adjustments made in preparing the accounting statements;
- explain the meaning of accruals and prepayments, and give examples of each;
- identify the effect of depreciation on a set of accounts;
- compare the two main methods of depreciation;
- calculate the effect of the adjustments on the income and expenditure account and balance sheet;
- contrast 'bad debts' and 'provision for doubtful debts';
- recognise these adjustments when included in statements;
- distinguish between the 'cash' and 'accruals' basis of accounting;
- explain the distinction between restricted, unrestricted and designated funds;
- identify the account items which are included in each statement.

---

A number of additional items appear in the final version of the income and expenditure account and the balance sheet. This is because these are **book-keeping adjustments** rather than amounts that have actually been paid or received.

These adjustments ensure that the income and expenditure account and balance sheet reflect the true picture of the NGO for the year concerned.

# BOOK-KEEPING ADJUSTMENTS

Common adjustments in accounting statements are:

1. **Closing stock**
2. **Accruals** and **prepayments**
3. **Depreciation**
4. **Bad debts** and the **provision for doubtful debts**

These adjustments were not included in the examples of the income and expenditure account and balance sheet shown in Chapter 5, Figures 16 and 17.

## 1. CLOSING STOCK

Items which have been purchased for use over a period of time, may not have been used up at the point at which the accounting period ends. There are likely to be some items left in stock.

In the Lomtaka Centre, for example, the drugs purchased may not have been used up by *the end of the first year*. If this is the case, the value of the items *actually* used during the year is needed to complete the income and expenditure account. This can be calculated as follows.

> Value of purchases of an item during the current period
> *less* value of closing stock of the item
> = amount used during the period and total included in the income and expenditure account *for that item*

The value of the closing stock is obtained by counting each item of stock on the last day of the accounting period, and calculating its value, based on *the lower of* either the cost price or what it is worth at the time. Some items may lose their value. Drugs, for example which are no longer safe to use, will be of no value. Each item's value should be compared with that in the stock records.

*In the second and subsequent years* of an organisation, there will be an opening as well as a closing stock included in the financial statements.

This will be calculated as follows.

> Value of opening stock of the item (that is last year's closing stock)
> *plus* value of purchases of an item during the current period
> *less* value of closing stock of the item
> = amount used during the period and total included in the income and
> expenditure account *for that item*

The value of the total closing stock for all the items together will be included as a current asset in the balance sheet.

---

## EXAMPLE 6.1

The unused stock of drugs held by Lomtaka Health Care Centre at 31 December (year 1), is valued at 10,129.00. The trial balance (Figure 15) shows that the amount of drugs purchased over the year up to 31 December (year 1) was 104,621.00.

1. What amount should be included for purchase of drugs in the income and expenditure account for year 1, as a result of this adjustment?
2. What figure would be included in the current assets section of the balance sheet for closing stock of drugs as at 31 December (year 1)?

*SOLUTION TO EXAMPLE 6.1*

1. *Income and expenditure account for year 1:*

| | | |
|---|---|---|
| Total purchase of drugs | = | 104,621.00 |
| Closing stock (unused) at 31 December | = | 10,129.00 |
| **Income and expenditure amount** | = | **94,492.00** |

2. *Balance sheet as at 31 December (year 1):*
   **Current assets**

| | |
|---|---|
| Closing stock of drugs | 10,129.00 |

---

## 2. ACCRUALS AND PREPAYMENTS

Accounting rules state that the income and expenditure account must include only expenses incurred and income earned for the period being considered, whether or not they have been paid or received during that period.

This means that all amounts that *should* have been paid or received in the period in question, must be taken into account. Amounts due for the activities of a period but for which an invoice has not been received and that are not settled until the following period are referred to as **accruals**. Amounts paid in the current period for activities in the following period are referred to as **prepayments**. Income received, but not yet due is called **income in advance**, and income due, but not yet received is called **income in arrears**.

In the *income and expenditure account*, accruals (*due but not yet paid*) are added to the appropriate expense item to show the full amount relating to the period being considered. Prepayments (*paid but not yet due*) are taken off the expense item to leave only the figure relating to the period under review. Income in advance (*received but not yet due*) is deducted from the income item, and income in arrears (*due but not yet received*) is added to the income item to leave just the amount of the accounts under review.

These adjustments should result in a full twelve months' income and expenditure!

In the *balance sheet*, accruals (*due but not yet paid*) are shown in the current liabilities, and prepayments (*paid but not yet due*) are shown in current assets. Income in advance (*received but not yet due*) is shown in current liabilities, and income in arrears (*due but not yet received*) is shown in current assets.

Remember that the object of these adjustments is to include only the amounts that *should* have been paid or received in the year being considered, and exclude anything from outside that year. This can be seen more clearly in the following example from the Lomtaka Centre.

---

## EXAMPLE 6.2

1.  What adjustments should be made to the figures in the draft income and expenditure account (year 1) shown in Figure 16 as a result of the following?

- The Centre has still to receive an invoice of 8,700.00 for the purchase of drugs used in the year to 31 December (year 1). Take into account the information given in *example 6.1* about the purchase of drugs and stock held at 31 December (year 1).

- An amount of 1,500.00 has been paid in advance in December (year 1), for medical supplies which will not be delivered and used until the following January (year 2).

- Fees and charges include an amount received in advance of treatment for 3,550.00. This treatment will be undertaken in the following financial year (year 2).

- Fees to trainers of 1,485.00 relating to year 1, are still unpaid at 31 December (year 1) (this is to be shown under the 'training programme' item).

- Donoraid was due to pay another 10,000.00 to the Centre during year 1. This will now be received in the following February (year 2).

2. Which items should be included in the current asset and current liabilities sections of the balance sheet at 31 December (year 1)?

## SOLUTION TO EXAMPLE 6.2

1. *Income and expenditure account for year 1:*
- Purchase of drugs | = | 104,621.00 from example 6.1

| | | | |
|---|---|---|---|
| Purchase of drugs | = | 104,621.00 | from example 6.1 |
| *less* stock at 31 December (year 1) | = | 10,129.00 | from example 6.1 |
| | | 94,492.00 | |
| *plus* unpaid amount, 31 December | = | 8,700.00 | |
| **Income and expenditure figure** | | **103,192.00** | |

| | | |
|---|---|---|
| Medical supplies | = | 61,309.00 |
| *less* prepayment | = | 1,500.00 |
| **Income and expenditure figure** | | **59,809.00** |

| | | |
|---|---|---|
| Fees and charges | = | 114,284.00 |
| *less* income in advance | = | 3,550.00 |
| **Income and expenditure figure** | | **110,734.00** |

| | | |
|---|---|---|
| Training programme | = | 5,293.00 |
| *plus* accrual | = | 1,485.00 |
| **Income and expenditure figure** | | **6,778.00** |

| | | |
|---|---|---|
| Donoraid donation | = | 240,000.00 |
| *plus* income in arrears | = | 10,000.00 |
| **Income and expenditure figure** | | **250,000.00** |

2. *Balance sheet as at 31 December (year 1):*

| | |
|---|---|
| **Current Assets** | |
| Prepayment | 1,500.00 |
| Income in arrears | 10,000.00 |
| | |
| *Less:* **Current Liabilities** | |
| Accruals | |
| (8,700 + 1,485) | 10,185.00 |
| Income in advance | 3,550.00 |

## 3. DEPRECIATION

The life of most fixed assets (for example vehicles or computers) is for a limited number of years, and depreciation is therefore calculated to:

- charge the value of the asset over its lifetime year by year to the income and expenditure account;
- reflect an estimated value of the asset (after each year's use) in the balance sheet.

Internationally, depreciation is calculated by two main methods:

### Straight line method
The **straight line method** is the easiest and, therefore the most widely used method of calculating depreciation.

The calculation is:    $$\frac{\text{Cost } less \text{ residual value}}{\text{Number of years}}$$

**Residual value** is the amount the asset is expected to be worth at the end of its useful life. This figure is often ignored in the calculation because it is so difficult to estimate! The number of years can be chosen by the NGO to reflect the length of time a particular asset is likely to last.

---

*Example:*
A computer is purchased for 80,000.00 and it is expected to last for 4 years. At the end of that time it is estimated that it will have a residual value of 5,000.00. The straight line calculation is as follows:

$$\text{Depreciation} \quad = \quad \frac{80,000.00 \; less \; 5,000.00}{4 \text{ years}}$$

$$= \quad 18,750.00 \text{ per year.}$$

---

### Reducing balance method
The reducing balance method is most appropriate for items which lose a large amount of their value in the first few years (for example, new vehicles). A percentage rate is assumed as the rate at which to charge depreciation. This can be determined by using a mathematical formula and if calculated accurately, the balance at the end of the period of years will be the residual value. It will be

assumed that this has been calculated to be 50% for the purposes of this example.

This fixed percentage (50%) of the *cost* is calculated in the first year. In the second and future years this percentage is multiplied by the *cost less the depreciation charged to date*.

---

***Example:***

Using the same information as in the straight line example shown above, and a percentage rate of 50%, the reducing balance calculation is as follows:

| | |
|---|---|
| Cost | 80,000.00 |
| Depreciation (year 1) | |
| (50% of 80,000.00) | 40,000.00 |
| | 40,000.00 |
| Depreciation (year 2) | |
| (50% of 40,000.00) | 20,000.00 |
| | 20,000.00 |
| Depreciation (year 3) | |
| (50% of 20,000.00) | 10,000.00 |
| | 10,000.00 |
| Depreciation (year 4) | |
| (50% of 10,000.00) | 5,000.00 |
| Residual value | 5,000.00 |

---

The current year's depreciation is shown in the income and expenditure account, as an expense.

The depreciation figure is also included in the balance sheet. This is the *total depreciation to date*, which is shown under the **fixed assets** section. In the balance sheet fixed assets section there are three figures shown for each asset – 'cost', '**total depreciation to date**' (the current year and any previous years' depreciation) and '**net book value**' (that is cost *less* total depreciation to date).

Example 6.3 shows how this will be presented for the Lomtaka Centre.

## EXAMPLE 6.3

The Lomtaka Centre is to calculate the depreciation for its fixed assets at the end of the first year.

The vehicle costs 15,298.00 and is expected to last 5 years. The reducing balance method of depreciation is to be used, at a rate of 60%.

The equipment costs 30,198.00 and is expected to last 5 years, with no residual value. The straight line basis of depreciation is to be used.

1. Calculate the depreciation for the first year, for the vehicle and the equipment.

2. Show how the fixed assets and depreciation would appear in the balance sheet as at 31 December (year 1), under the following headings:

| Fixed assets | Cost | Total Depreciation to Date | Net Book Value* |
|---|---|---|---|
| Vehicle | | | |
| Equipment | _____ | _____ | _____ |
| | _____ | _____ | |

* net book value = cost *less* total depreciation to date.
All calculations are made to the nearest whole number.

### SOLUTION TO EXAMPLE 6.3 ( year 1)

1. **Vehicle using reducing balance method**
   15,298.00 x 60% = 9,179.00   (to the nearest whole number)

   **Equipment using straight line method**
   30,198.00 ÷ 5 years = 6,040.00   (to the nearest whole number)

2. **Balance sheet as at 31 December (year 1):**

| Fixed assets | Cost | Total Depreciation to Date | Net Book Value |
|---|---|---|---|
| Vehicle | 15,298 | 9,179 | 6,119 |
| Equipment | 30,198 | 6,040 | 24,158 |
| | 45,496 | 15,219 | 30,277 |

Note: no line is placed under the total of 'net book value'. This is because this total is added to others in the balance sheet. The totals of the 'cost' and 'depreciation to date' columns are there merely for information.

At the end of the second year, the depreciation on the assets, shown in example 6.3, will include the depreciation at the end of the first year, plus depreciation charges in the second year. The table as at 31 December (year 2), *if no items were bought or sold*, would look like this.

---

**YEAR 2 – EXTRACT FROM FIXED ASSETS SECTION OF BALANCE SHEET WITHOUT FURTHER PURCHASES OR SALES OF FIXED ASSETS**

| Fixed assets | Cost | Total Depreciation to Date | Net Book Value |
|---|---|---|---|
| Vehicle | 15,298 | 12,850 (note 1) | 2,448 |
| Equipment | 30,198 | 12,080 (note 2) | 18,118 |
| | 45,496 | 24,930 | 20,566 |

Note 1: 6,119.00 (net book value, year 1) x 60% = 3,671.00 (year 2)
  3,671.00 + 9,179.00 (year 1) =      12,850.00
  (to nearest whole number)

Note 2: 6,040.00 (year 1) + 6,040.00 (year 2) = 12,080.00

---

**Figure 18: Extract of the Lomtaka Centre's year 2 balance sheet to show the effects of depreciation**

Depreciation calculations are often kept in a **fixed assets register**. This lists the details and value of items purchased, the amount of depreciation for each year and the net book value.

### Ensuring money is available to buy a new item
*Depreciation is merely a book-keeping entry – no money changes hands!*

The effect of including depreciation in the income and expenditure account is to reduce the amount of the excess of income over expenditure or surplus figure (or increase a deficit). This may result in the NGO thinking it has a smaller surplus, and so it is more careful, *but it will not in itself ensure there is money available to buy a new item when the current one is no longer of use.*
*If it is essential that funds are available to replace the current vehicle, for example, a transfer of 'real money' from the bank account to a separate* **savings account** *is required.* This is *in addition* to allowing for depreciation in the accounts. Indeed the amount transferred will need to be for more than the amount of the depreciation each year, as the replacement cost will usually be higher than the cost of the original item! If this transfer is made, money will move from the bank current account to a new bank savings account. Current

assets on the balance sheet will reflect this transfer.

## Depreciation in NGOs

Small NGOs do not usually provide for depreciation, and if they do they often do not provide a savings account. Donors also vary in the level to which they allow their donations to be used to fund depreciation in the accounting statements.

Some organisations write off the whole of the value of an asset in the year of purchase, in a similar way to including the full cost of the item in the receipts and payments account. This is appropriate if a new asset (say a vehicle) is, on average, purchased yearly – the overall effect would then be the same. For example, depreciating one-fifth of the value of each of five vehicles in a year, is the same as writing off the value of the whole of one vehicle each year. (Try working it out!) However, if such an asset is purchased only occasionally, writing off the whole value in one year would distort the surplus/deficit figure in the income and expenditure account in that particular year.

Depreciation is all about good management and it encourages the continued existence of an NGO. The transfer of money to a savings account may not always be possible and a donor may not be willing to fund this. If however a savings account is not created, a donor might be approached again and asked to donate a new vehicle, when the current one is no longer road worthy.

## 4. BAD DEBTS

The fourth adjustment to the trial balance is for **bad debts**. Bad debts describes the value of an NGO's debtors that, for some reason (for example bankruptcy of the person owing the money), will not be received. Debtors appear in the accounts only if **credit** terms have been allowed – someone who owes money has been allowed to pay at a later date. Debtors will occur when sales are made on credit. If an organisation has no debtors, no adjustment for bad debts is necessary.

'Bad debts' accounting falls into two categories.

## Bad debts which are known

It is usual to review outstanding debtors regularly to make sure that all payment of invoices has been received. Those which are unpaid and quite old may never be received. A senior person must decide how likely this is and authorise the deletion of the debts from the accounts. These are then treated as 'bad debts' *for accounting purposes*. It may however still be possible to try and obtain the amount owing! Bad debts are treated as an *expense* in the income and expenditure account.

The accounting for this is as follows.

- If 'bad debts' are included in the trial balance (because they have been adjusted *during* the year), this figure has already reduced the debtors' figure. No further action is needed, other than including them in the income and expenditure account.
- If however, it is decided to charge bad debts to the income and expenditure account *after* the trial balance has been prepared, they are not included in the ledger. The debtors' figure in the trial balance therefore needs to be reduced by the amount of bad debts.

## Bad debts which are not known

NGOs with a high debtors figure know from experience that they are likely to have a certain percentage of their debtors who will not pay, but they do not know precisely which ones they are. They therefore include an estimated figure as a provision for doubtful debts. This will be based on past experience and will usually be calculated as a percentage of total debtors.

The accounting for this is as follows.

- Include an increase in the provision for doubtful debts as an expense in the income and expenditure account.
- Reduce the debtors' figure by the total amount of the provision and show this in the balance sheet.
- Bad debts which are known and adjusted *after the trial balance has been prepared*, reduce the debtors' figure *prior* to the provision for bad debts being calculated.

## EXAMPLE 6.4

At the end of year 1, debtors owe the Lomtaka Centre 23,310.00. It is estimated that 280.00 of this total will not be received by the Centre, and needs to be charged as bad debts. The Centre is to make a provision for doubtful debts of 3% of the *remaining* debtors in case there is future non-payment.

Show the entries needed in the income and expenditure account and on the balance sheet for year 1. All calculations should be to the nearest whole number.

### SOLUTION TO EXAMPLE 6.4
*Entries in the income and expenditure account (year 1):*
Bad debts written off        =     280.00

| | | | |
|---|---|---|---|
| Debtors | = | 23,310.00 | workings only – not |
| *less* bad debts written off | = | 280.00 | included in income and |
| Revised debtors figure | | 23,030.00 | expenditure account |

Provision for doubtful debts
(23,030.00 x 3%)                  =      691.00 (to the nearest whole number)

*Entries in the balance sheet as at 31 December (year 1):*
**Current Assets**
Debtors   (23,310.00 *less* 280.00)    =    23,030.00
*Less* provision for doubtful debtors   =     691.00        22,339.00

### Bad debts in NGOs
Not all NGOs have 'bad debts' or a 'provision for bad debts' in their accounts. Indeed some will find they have very few people who owe them money. However, if there is a large number of debtors, it is essential to review the amounts outstanding to try and ensure payment or, if they will not pay, to reduce the debtors figure. If 'bad debts' or 'provision for bad debts' appear in the statements it indicates that someone is undertaking such a review.

# USING THE ADJUSTMENTS FROM EXAMPLES 6.1 TO 6.4 TO PRODUCE THE FINAL VERSION OF THE INCOME AND EXPENDITURE ACCOUNT AND BALANCE SHEET

These adjustments can be summarised as follows.

- At 31 December (year 1), the unused closing stock of drugs is valued at 10,129.00.

- An invoice of 8,700.00 has still to be received for the purchase of drugs, used in the year to 31 December (year 1).

- An amount of 1,500.00 has been paid in advance in December (year 1) for medical supplies which will not be delivered or used until the following January (year 2).

- Fees and charges include an amount received in advance of treatment for 3,550.00.

- Fees to trainers of 1,485.00 relating to year 1, are still unpaid at 31 December (year 1).

- Donoraid is due to pay another 10,000.00 to the Centre during year 1. This will be received in the following February (year 2).

- The vehicle costs 15,298.00 and is expected to last for 5 years. The reducing balance method of depreciation is to be used, at a rate of 60%.

- The equipment costs 30,198.00 and is expected to last 5 years, with no residual value. The straight line method of depreciation is to be used.

- Of the total debtors of 23,310.00, it is estimated that 280.00 of this total will not be received by the Centre and needs to be charged as a 'bad debts' expense.

- The Centre is to make a provision for doubtful debts of 3% of the *remaining* debtors in case there is future non-payment.

**Figure 19: Summary of adjustments to the first draft of the Lomtaka Centre's income and expenditure account and balance sheet**

With these adjustments included, the final version of the income and expenditure account and balance sheet will be as follows:

**Lomtaka Health Care Centre: Income and Expenditure account for the period ended 31 December (year 1) – FINAL VERSION**

**Income**

| | | |
|---|---|---|
| Grants | - WEV | 100,000 |
| | - Donoraid (240,000 + 10,000) | 250,000 |
| Department of Health | | 350,000 |
| Fees and charges (114,284 *less* 3,550) | | 110,734 |
| Other income | | 20,023 |
| | | 830,757 |

**Expenditure**

| | | |
|---|---|---|
| Salaries | 483,109 | |
| Rent of premises | 96,000 | |
| Purchase of drugs | | |
| (104,621 *less* 10,129 [closing stock] | | |
|       + 8,700 [amount outstanding]) | 103,192 | |
| Medical supplies (61,309 *less* 1,500) | 59,809 | |
| Electricity | 11,547 | |
| Travelling expenses | 18,394 | |
| Training programme (5,293 + 1,485) | 6,778 | |
| Office costs (including audit) | 10,887 | |
| Other payments | 2,192 | |
| Depreciation   - equipment (30,198 ÷ 5) | 6,040 | |
|             - vehicle (15,298 x 60%) | 9,179 | |
| Bad debts written off | 280 | |
| Provision for doubtful debts | | |
| (23,310 *less* 280 [bad debts] = 23,030 x 3%) | 691 | 808,098 |
| **Excess of income over expenditure** | | **22,659** |

Note: Figures are rounded to the nearest whole number.

**Figure 20: Final version of the Lomtaka Centre's income and expenditure account (year 1)**

## KEY POINTS FROM THE INCOME AND EXPENDITURE ACCOUNT

• This income and expenditure account includes all the adjustments, and thus reflects the activities of the Centre for a 12-month period.

- Adjustments have been made for stock, income and expenditure in arrears or in advance, depreciation and bad debts.
- The figures in this statement can therefore be confidently compared with the budget, as they are comparing 'like with like'.
- The 10,000.00 added to the Donoraid donation would in fact only be added if, as in this example, the organisation were confident that the money would be received in the next financial year.
- The excess of income over expenditure is now 22,659.00. Compare this with the previous excess of income over expenditure of 30,955.00 before the adjustments were made (Chapter 5, Figure 16).

| **Lomtaka Health Care Centre: Balance Sheet as at 31 December (year 1)** **FINAL VERSION** | | | |
|---|---|---|---|
| **Fixed Assets** | **Cost** | **Total Depreciation to Date** | **Net Book Value** (cost *less* total dep'n) |
| Vehicle | 15,298 | 9,179 | 6,119 |
| Equipment | 30,198 | 6,040 | 24,158 |
| | 45,496 | 15,219 | 30,277 |
| **Current Assets** | | | |
| Closing stock of drugs | | 10,129 | |
| Debtors (23,310 *less* 280) | 23,030 | | |
| *Less* provision for doubtful debts | 691 | 22,339 | |
| Prepayment (payment in advance) | | 1,500 | |
| Income in arrears | | 10,000 | |
| Bank and cash | | 30,385 | |
| | | 74,353 | |
| **Less: Current Liabilities** | | | |
| Creditors | 13,236 | | |
| Accruals (payments in arrears) (8,700 + 1,485) | 10,185 | | |
| Income in advance | 3,550 | 26,971 | |
| *Working capital (current assets less current liabilities)* | | | 47,382 |
| | | | 77,659 |
| **Less: Long-term Liabilities** | | | |
| Bank loan | | | 10,000 |
| | | | 67,659 |
| *Financed by:* **Accumulated Fund** | | | |
| Capital grant – Department of Health | | | 45,000 |
| *Plus*: Excess of income over expenditure | | | 22,659 |
| | | | 67,659 |
| Note: Figures are rounded to the nearest whole number. | | | |

**Figure 21: Final version of the Lomtaka Centre's balance sheet (year 1)**

## KEY POINTS FROM THE BALANCE SHEET

- The cost, total depreciation to date and the net book value are shown in full (some financial statements would include the detailed information as a note).
- The headings 'cost', 'total depreciation to date' and 'net book value' *refer only to the section on fixed assets*. They are not headings for the whole balance sheet. The fixed asset figure actually used in the balance sheet calculation is the *total net book value* (30,277.00), the figures for 'cost' and 'total depreciation to date' are given merely for information.
- The two columns of figures below *cost* and *total depreciation to date*, are there to provide more detail about the totals in the right hand column. For example the current assets (74,353.00) less the current liabilities (26,971.00) gives a total of 47,382.00 for the working capital figure in the right hand column.
- The debtors' figure has been adjusted for the bad debts written off (not always shown in the balance sheet), and the provision for doubtful debts. These items may be shown as a note to the accounts.
- *Prepayments* and *income in arrears* are shown as part of current assets – these are amounts (in effect) owed to the Lomtaka Centre at the date of the balance sheet. *Accruals* and *income in advance* are shown as current liabilities – these are amounts owed by the Centre.
- The bank loan is shown as part of long-term liabilities. The rule is that it is included here if the loan is repayable after one year. If repayable in less than a year, the loan would be included as part of current liabilities.
- The accumulated fund shows the capital grant plus this year's surplus only, as this is the Lomtaka Centre's first year of operation.

## 'CASH' OR 'ACCRUALS' BASIS OF ACCOUNTING

The distinction between the receipts and payments and the income and expenditure accounts described in Chapter 5, are sometimes referred to by the shorthand form of **cash accounting** or **accruals accounting**. Cash accounting refers to the contents of the receipts and payments account being merely cash (and bank), but having no accounting adjustments. The income and expenditure account however contains adjustments one of which is an adjustment for accruals, hence the name.

The accounting policies or notes to the accounts will often state which accounting basis has been used. Some organisations may, confusingly, describe an 'income and expenditure account' as being compiled on a 'cash accounting' basis. If this is the case, then no adjustments will have been made, and the statement will be what has been described in this book as a receipts and payments account! These two terms 'cash' and 'accruals' help to provide a clear indication of the accounting basis used irrespective of the name used for the accounting statement.

# FUND ACCOUNTING, RESTRICTED AND DESIGNATED FUNDS

Many NGOs are given funds for a particular purpose and, as such, these amounts need to be accounted for separately. Some NGOs may consider opening separate bank accounts but usually this is unnecessary if the accounting for the money is clearly identified.

Similar but different terms are used to identify funds.

**Restricted funds** refer to money given by a donor for a particular purpose which can only be used for that purpose. The opposite of this is **unrestricted funds** which is money that can be used for any expenditure within the NGO. These funds must not be confused and the accounting needs to be separate.

**Designated funds** are part of the unrestricted funds which the NGO itself has decided to identify in a particular way, for example for the purchase of a new computer system. These funds can be undesignated at a later date if required.

Special 'flagging' may be needed in the accounts to ensure that income and expenditure items are correctly identified. This is sometimes described as **fund accounting**. If the funding is for a few specific items, for example the purchase of new vehicles, it will not be difficult to find these items in the accounting system and report back on them easily.

However, if the funding is for large or complex activities, for example an emergency relief programme, it will be essential to ensure that the accounting system can trace all transactions and automatically list them together in the same order as the donor's budget. It is often worthwhile consulting a qualified accountant in order to prepare such a system at the very beginning of this kind of programme.

The income and expenditure account itself can be prepared to show separate columns for restricted and unrestricted funds. This is a legal requirement, for example, for larger charities in the UK.

If, at the date of the balance sheet a restricted amount is unspent, it will be shown in the 'financed by' part of the balance sheet, under accumulated funds. This recognises that the donation, or part of it, has still to be spent.

# WHICH ITEM GOES IN WHICH ACCOUNT?

The contents of the income and expenditure account and the balance sheet can be seen as a division between *capital* and *revenue*. The capital items (assets, liabilities and accumulated fund) appear in the balance sheet. The revenue items (income and expenses) appear in the income and expenditure account.

The following summary gives examples of items included in each account.

---

**ITEMS INCLUDED IN THE INCOME AND EXPENDITURE ACCOUNT AND THE BALANCE SHEET**

| **INCOME AND EXPENDITURE ACCOUNT** | **BALANCE SHEET** |
|---|---|
| INCOME | LAND AND BUILDINGS |
|   GRANTS | VEHICLES |
|   FEES AND CHARGES | EQUIPMENT / MACHINERY |
|   OTHER INCOME | COMPUTERS |
|   *EFFECT OF INCOME IN ARREARS* |   *LESS* PROVISION FOR |
|     *AND INCOME IN ADVANCE* |   DEPRECIATION |
| | CLOSING STOCK |
| EXPENDITURE | DEBTORS |
|   SALARIES | PREPAYMENTS |
|   RENT | INCOME IN ARREARS |
|   TRAVEL COSTS | BANK |
|   AIR FARES | CASH |
|   OFFICE EXPENSES | CREDITORS |
|   DEPRECIATION CHARGE | ACCRUALS |
|   BAD DEBTS / PROVISION | INCOME IN ADVANCE |
|   OTHER EXPENDITURE | LOANS |
|   *EFFECT OF ACCRUALS AND* | ACCUMULATED FUND |
|     *PREPAYMENTS* | |

---

**Figure 22: Identification of the items which are included in either the income and expenditure account or the balance sheet**

# Chapter 7

## Accounting for Income-generating or Commercial Organisations

---

**OBJECTIVES OF THIS CHAPTER**

This chapter introduces the accounts for income-generating or commercial organisations that replace the statements already examined. This includes the trading and profit and loss accounts which will enable the calculation of a profit figure.

Having considered the material and worked through the examples in this chapter, you should be able to:

- explain what is included in a trading and profit and loss account;
- calculate the 'cost of goods sold figure' from information provided;
- identify differences in terminology and format between these accounts and their not-for-profit equivalents;
- recognise trading and profit and loss accounts.

---

NGOs are not always not-for-profit. Income-generating activities, for example, usually aim to make a profit, and their accounting needs are slightly different.

The *process* of accounting for commercial activities is the same as described in Chapters 4 and 5. Business organisations however replace the income and expenditure account by the following accounts.

- a **trading account** (if the organisation is buying and selling goods);
- a **profit and loss account**.

*These accounts are often combined into one*, described as the trading and profit and loss account, or sometimes simply as the profit and loss account.

# TRADING AND PROFIT AND LOSS ACCOUNT FOR AN INCOME-GENERATING OR COMMERCIAL ORGANISATION

Businesses which buy and sell goods for resale will usually include a trading account at the beginning of their profit and loss account. This identifies the profit made purely on the buying and selling of goods.

This account is presented in the following format.

| Tzabana Income-Generating Company | | |
|---|---|---|
| Trading account for the period ended 30 September | | |
| Sales | | 44,741 |
| | | |
| *Less:* cost of goods sold | | |
| | | |
| Opening stock | 5,890 | |
| *Plus:* purchases | 19,971 | |
| | 25,861 | |
| | | |
| *Less:* closing stock | 2,190 | 23,671 |
| | | |
| **Gross profit** | | **21,070** |

**Figure 23: Example of a trading account**

## KEY POINTS FROM THE TRADING ACCOUNT

- The purpose of the trading account is to calculate the **gross profit** of a business. This is the profit related purely to the trading activity, and before any other expenses are deducted.
- The two columns are to provide a sub-total of the **cost of goods sold** figure (23,671.00).
- The cost of goods sold provides the cost value of the items included in the sales figure. This will comprise any opening stock, *plus* what has been purchased during the year and *less* any closing stock not yet sold at the end of the year.

The expenses of running the business are deducted in the profit and loss account. This calculates the profit for the whole business activities using the gross profit, calculated in the trading account, as its starting point. The profit and loss account is presented in the following format.

| Tzabana Income-Generating Company Profit and Loss account for the period ended 30 September | | |
|---|---|---|
| Gross profit | | 21,070 |
| *Less:* expenses | | |
| Rent | 3,540 | |
| Vehicle expenses | 1,445 | |
| Salaries | 4,758 | |
| Depreciation | 4,171 | |
| Miscellaneous expenses | 4,210 | 18,124 |
| **Net profit** | | **2,946** |

**Figure 24: Example of a profit and loss account**

## KEY POINTS FROM THE PROFIT AND LOSS ACCOUNT

- The purpose of the profit and loss account is to calculate the **net profit** figure.
- The two columns are again only to provide a sub-total for the expenses.
- As in the income and expenditure account these expenses may have been adjusted for accruals and prepayments (see Chapters 5 and 6). Bad debts and provision for doubtful debts adjustments have not been included in the examples in this chapter.
- The net profit figure will be added to the **capital** section in the balance sheet, in the same way as the excess of income over expenditure is added to the accumulated funds in not-for-profit organisations.

# BALANCE SHEET FOR AN INCOME-GENERATING OR COMMERCIAL ORGANISATION

The balance sheets for income-generating or commercial organisations will look similar to those in not-for-profit organisations, but the terminology is slightly different. **Capital**, for example, is the term likely to be used instead of the 'accumulated fund' in the income and expenditure account. Capital represents the amount of money originally put into a business by its owner(s) plus previous years' profits and less any previous years' losses.

| **Tzabana Income-Generating Company** | | | |
|---|---|---|---|
| **Balance Sheet as at 30 September** | | | |
| **Fixed assets** | Cost | Total Depreciation to Date | Net Book Value (cost *less* total dep'n) |
| Land and building | 175,004 | - | 175,004 |
| Vehicles | 32,640 | 9,385 | 23,255 |
| Equipment | 8,209 | 2,052 | 6,157 |
|  | 215,853 | 11,437 | 204,416 |
| **Current assets** | | | |
| Closing stock | | 28,351 | |
| Debtors | | 13,293 | |
| Bank and cash | | 36,207 | |
|  | | 77,851 | |
| *Less:* **Current liabilities** | | | |
| Creditors | | 21,393 | 56,458 |
|  | | | 260,874 |
| *Less:* **Long-term liabilities** | | | |
| Bank loan | | | 10,000 |
|  | | | 250,874 |
| Financed by: | | | |
| **Opening capital** (at previous 1 October) | | | 247,928 |
| *Plus:* **net profit** (from profit and loss account) | | | 2,946 |
| **Closing capital** (at 30 September) | | | 250,874 |

**Figure 25: Example of a balance sheet for a trading organisation**

## KEY POINTS FROM THE BALANCE SHEET

- The balance sheet format is similar in all organisations, although the layout is subject to international variations (examples are shown in Appendix C).
- Land and buildings have not been depreciated. This is common practice in many countries.

- The term capital is used to indicate money invested in the business by the owner(s) in place of the not-for-profit 'accumulated fund'.
- The net profit (from the profit and loss account) is added to the capital. This is, in effect, the equivalent of 'interest' earned by the people who invested their money as capital.
- The net profit may be shared amongst the owners (or shareholders if the organisation is a company). Here the net profit has all been left in the business.
- The interpretation of these statements is similar to that shown in Chapters 8 and 9. Income-generating or commercial organisations will be particularly interested in the level of the gross and net profit figures.

# Chapter 8

## Interpretation of Accounting Statements

---

**OBJECTIVES OF THIS CHAPTER**

This chapter looks at the interpretation of accounts using the Lomtaka Centre's accounts as an example. Examining accounts raises questions that NGOs may wish to ask themselves, or that a donor may wish to resolve. A checklist in Appendix A gives a structured approach to this analysis.

Having considered the material and worked through the examples in this chapter and the checklist in Appendix A, you should be able to:

- compare an accounting statement for two years and ask appropriate questions;
- compare the accounting statement with the budget and ask appropriate questions;
- illustrate how knowledge of the accounting policies and notes to the accounts can help to interpret the statements;
- use a checklist to assist in the analysis of accounting statements.

---

Accounting or financial statements (that is budgets, the receipt and payment, income and expenditure or profit and loss accounts and the balance sheet) reveal a great deal about an organisation. Accountants can glean valuable information from statements and other accounting records, and it is possible for a non-specialist to learn the key indicators.

The use made of this information will help to answer the following questions:

- Will all the organisational objectives be achieved?
- Will the organisation be able to pay all its debts?
- What kind of support is most appropriate?
- How effective are the organisational systems of financial management?
- Can the organisation be financially sustainable in the long term?

Although the interpretation from the financial statements is not the only factor to consider in deciding how best to request or provide support, to ignore it means that vital information is missed in the decision-making process.

# USES AND LIMITATIONS OF ANNUAL STATEMENTS

The annual accounting statements are usually produced several months after the end of the year. As such they are of limited use in *controlling* the financial state of an organisation as this needs to be based on an up-to-date version of the budget and actual statement.

The annual statements however are able to provide an overview of the NGO, to show what is contained in the audit report and to compare retrospectively a full year's income and expenditure with the budget. The balance sheet presented in the annual statements may be seen only once a year and so is particularly important. Figures in this can be compared over a number of years to reveal trends. Annual statements may be the only information made available to those outside the NGO.

Information from the annual accounting statements can give new insights into an NGO's management and, together with non-financial data, builds up a comprehensive picture to inform decision-making.

# A STARTING POINT

In addition to managers, a number of other people need to interpret accounting information. The governing body, donors and other stakeholders may all require clarification of the data and will want to ask questions about it. The clearer the information produced, the less questions will be asked!

When examining a set of accounts it is helpful to develop a 'questioning' approach. Look at the information and try and justify any changes. If this is not possible, it is worth asking questions about these particular points. If the answers are still unclear, it is probably worth seeking advice from a qualified accountant.

To gain a full picture it is helpful to compare the figures in a set of financial accounts with the

- current budget;
- following year's budget (if available);
- corresponding figures in the previous year's accounts.

The following examples go through some of the usual statements, making suggestions for the kinds of question that could be asked.

## EXAMPLE 8. 1: COMPARING AN INCOME AND EXPENDITURE ACCOUNT WITH TWO YEARS' BUDGETS

The Lomtaka Centre accounts for year 1 will be analysed, and questions raised. This version of the income and expenditure account, contains the budgeted figures for years 1 and 2.

*The information in the income and expenditure account used here, is exactly the same as in Chapter 6.* However, the *presentation* is slightly different to the format of the income and expenditure account shown in Figure 20. Before comparing and interpreting the amounts, try to identify the differences in presentation! Both formats are commonly used throughout the world.

| **Lomtaka Health Care Centre: Income and Expenditure account for the period ended 31 December (year 1)** | | | |
|---|---|---|---|
| **Budget year 1** | | **Year 1** | **Budget year 2** |
| | **Income** | | |
| 100,000 | Grants  - WEV | 100,000 | 100,000 |
| 250,000 | - Donoraid | 250,000 | 300,000 |
| 350,000 | Department of Health | 350,000 | 450,000 |
| 124,000 | Fees and charges | 110,734 | 139,080 |
| - | Other income | 20,023 | - |
| 824,000 | | 830,757 | 989,080 |
| | **Expenditure** | | |
| 467,130 | Salaries | 483,109 | 529,200 |
| 96,000 | Rent of premises | 96,000 | 120,000 |
| 132,000 | Purchase of drugs | 103,192 | 145,200 |
| 64,560 | Medical supplies | 59,809 | 71,016 |
| 12,840 | Electricity | 11,547 | 14,124 |
| 20,070 | Travelling expenses | 18,394 | 30,000 |
| 5,000 | Training programme | 6,778 | 17,000 |
| 11,400 | Office costs (including audit) | 10,887 | 12,540 |
| - | Other payments | 2,192 | - |
| 15,000 | Depreciation - equipment | 6,040 | 50,000 |
| | - vehicle | 9,179 | |
| - | Bad debts written off | 280 | - |
| - | Provision for doubtful debts | 691 | - |
| 824,000 | | 808,098 | 989,080 |
| **0** | **Excess of income over expenditure** | **22,659** | **0** |

**Figure 26: Lomtaka Centre's income and expenditure account (year 1) with budget figures for years 1 and 2**

## KEY POINTS FROM THE INTERPRETATION OF THE INCOME AND EXPENDITURE ACCOUNT AND BUDGETS

The statements in this example are interpreted by comparing the budget for the two years with the 'actual' figures of the income and expenditure account. The data from the income and expenditure account is, in effect, being used as a 'budget and actual statement' for the whole year, although it contains more complete information. This is because the finance staff will have made sure that the income and expenditure year-end account figures are accurate. The **accruals** and **prepayments** and other book-keeping adjustments will have been adjusted at the year end.

This example also includes year 2's budget for comparison. This is the kind of information that is compared internally within an organisation, and often shared with donors.

*The following are some general questions and comments from Example 8.1:*

- How well is the organisation achieving its objectives? (See also the narrative report.)
- How long ago was the year end? Having the income and expenditure account already prepared would indicate that it is at least a few months since the year end. If so, the budget for year 2 is likely to have already been partly used.
- How up to date is the accounting system generally?
- There are no notes explaining major differences for the items. Can they be provided?
- Who is responsible for monitoring the budget?
- Has a cash budget been prepared for next year?
- Has the income and expenditure account been audited? Fee paid in the income and expenditure account, but where is the audit report?
- If you are a member of the governing body or a donor do the statements represent your experience of the NGO?
- If you are one of the donors, do your records agree with what is shown here?
- Were any of these grants given for a specific purpose and have they been so used?
- Are all the calculations correct?
- Depreciation is included, but what will happen when the assets wear out? Has money been set aside for eventual replacement in the balance sheet?
- Bad debts adjustments indicates that a systematic review of debtors is carried out.

When looking at a 'budget and actual statement' we might also expect to see a comparison of the capital budget. However, comparing the budget with the income and expenditure account implies that there is a balance sheet, where the capital items should have been included. It would be important to see this.

The following 'working sheet' approach identifies *further questions* to ask. It is a quick and convenient way to collate the appropriate questions needed around the outside of the accounting statement itself. These notes can form the basis of questions to raise in a meeting or the contents of a letter asking for further information.

# WORKING SHEET FOR THE INCOME AND EXPENDITURE ACCOUNT WITH TWO YEARS' BUDGETS

*QUESTIONS TO ASK*

*Compare with narrative report.*

*What is the 'other income'? Can we have a breakdown? Why is there nothing in the budget for year 2?*

*Need breakdown of 'other payments'. Why not in year 2 budget?*

*Why so low for purchase of drugs and medical supplies? Why will it increase so much in year 2?*

*Why did year 1 expenditure stay within budget? Has 'other income' any relation to this?*

*Will year 2 income budget be reached? Evidence for this?*

**Lomtaka Health Care Centre: Income and Expenditure account for the period ended 31 December (year 1)**

| Budget year 1 | | Year 1 | Budget year 2 |
|---:|:---|---:|---:|
| | **Income** | | |
| 100,000 | Grants - WEV | 100,000 | 100,000 |
| 250,000 |        - Donoraid | 250,000 | 300,000 |
| 350,000 | Department of Health | 350,000 | 450,000 |
| 124,000 | Fees and charges | 110,734 | 139,080 |
| - | Other income | 20,023 | - |
| 824,000 | | 830,757 | 989,080 |
| | **Expenditure** | | |
| 467,130 | Salaries | 483,109 | 529,200 |
| 96,000 | Rent of premises | 96,000 | 120,000 |
| 132,000 | Purchase of drugs | 103,192 | 145,200 |
| 64,560 | Medical supplies | 59,809 | 71,016 |
| 12,840 | Electricity | 11,547 | 14,124 |
| 20,070 | Travelling expenses | 18,394 | 30,000 |
| 5,000 | Training programme | 6,778 | 17,000 |
| 11,400 | Office costs (including audit) | 10,887 | 12,540 |
| - | Other payments | 2,192 | - |
| 15,000 | Depreciation - equipment | 6,040 | 50,000 |
| |        - vehicle | 9,179 | |
| - | Bad debts written off | 280 | - |
| - | Provision for doubtful debts | 691 | - |
| 824,000 | | 808,098 | 989,080 |
| **0** | **Excess of income over expenditure** | **22,659** | **0** |

*Why were salaries in year 1 higher than budget? Increments? How does this compare with inflation? How has year 2 been calculated?*

*How realistic is nil 'excess' in year 2?*

*Why will electricity increase so much in year 2?*

*Travel not as high as expected? Why large increase in year 2? How calculated? Is round figure OK?*

*Training–what's included in year 2?*

*How do the increases in year 2 budget relate to inflation level?*

*Good that bad debts included. Is any estimate included for year 2?*

## EXAMPLE 8.2: COMPARING TWO YEARS' INCOME AND EXPENDITURE ACCOUNTS AND BALANCE SHEETS

In this example the Lomtaka Centre accounts for year 1 and year 2 (not previously seen!) will be analysed, and questions raised.

The *information* in the income and expenditure account and balance sheet used here, is the same as in Chapter 6. However, the *presentation* is slightly different to the format of the income and expenditure account and balance sheet shown in Figures 20 and 21. **Accounting policies** and **notes to the accounts** have been added in this presentation. The accounting policies explain how some of the figures have been calculated. The notes take some of the figures out of the statements to avoid too much detail.

**Lomtaka Health Care Centre: Income and Expenditure account for the period ended 31 December (years 1 and 2)**

| Year 1 | | | Year 2 |
|---|---|---|---|
| | **Income** | | |
| 100,000 | Grants - WEV | | 100,000 |
| 250,000 | - Donoraid | | 300,000 |
| 350,000 | Department of Health | | 450,000 |
| 110,734 | Fees and charges | | 122,673 |
| 20,023 | Other income | | 4,537 |
| 830,757 | | | 977,210 |
| | **Expenditure** | | |
| 483,109 | Salaries | 541,748 | |
| 96,000 | Rent of premises | 120,000 | |
| 103,192 | Purchase of drugs | 126,256 | |
| 59,809 | Medical supplies | 74,768 | |
| 11,547 | Electricity | 13,486 | |
| 18,394 | Travelling expenses | 27,471 | |
| 6,778 | Training programme | 18,732 | |
| 10,887 | Office costs (including audit) | 13,791 | |
| 2,192 | Other payments | 962 | |
| 15,219 | Depreciation | 49,793 | |
| 971 | Re: Bad debts (note 4) | 638 | 987,645 |
| 808,098 | | | |
| **22,659** | **Excess of income over expenditure** | | **(10,435)** |
| | **(Excess of expenditure over income)** | | |

**Figure 27: Lomtaka Centre's income and expenditure accounts (years 1 and 2)**

## KEY POINTS FROM THE INTERPRETATION OF THE TWO YEARS' INCOME AND EXPENDITURE ACCOUNTS

*The following are some general questions and comments.*

- Have the accounts been audited? The fee seems to have been paid but no audit report is with the accounts.
- If you are a manager, a member of the governing body or a donor, have you seen the fixed assets being used in the organisation?
- If you are a donor, do your records agree with the amounts received shown here?
- Were any of these grants given for a specific purpose and have they been so used?
- Are all the calculations correct?
- Depreciation is included, but what will happen when the assets wear out? No money appears to be set aside for eventual replacement.
- Bad debts adjustments indicate that a systematic review of debtors is carried out.
- Other questions are raised on the 'working sheet' on page 94.

**Lomtaka Health Care Centre: Balance Sheets as at 31 December (year 1 and 2)**

| Year 1 | | Year 2 |
|---|---|---|
| | **Fixed Assets** (note 1) | |
| 6,119 | Vehicles - net book value | 29,170 |
| 24,158 | Equipment - net book value | 18,118 |
| 30,277 | | 47,288 |
| | **Current Assets** | |
| 10,129 | Closing stock of drugs | 6,203 |
| 33,839 | Debtors (note 2) | 35,199 |
| 30,385 | Bank and cash | 63,113 |
| 74,353 | | 104,515 |
| | *Less:* **Current Liabilities** | |
| (26,971) | Creditors (note 3) | (17,775) |
| 47,382 | *Working capital (current assets less current liabilities)* | 86,740 |
| | *Less:* **Long-term Liabilities** | |
| (10,000) | Bank loan | (10,000) |
| **67,659** | | **124,028** |
| | *Financed by:* | |
| | **Accumulated Fund** | |
| - | Balance brought forward | 67,659 |
| 45,000 | Capital grant - Department of Health | 66,804 |
| 22,659 | *Plus:* Excess of income over expenditure | (10,435) |
| | (Excess of expenditure over income) | |
| **67,659** | | **124,028** |

**Figure 28: Lomtaka Centre's balance sheets (years 1 and 2)**

## KEY POINTS FROM THE INTERPRETATION OF THE TWO YEARS' BALANCE SHEETS

- Many of the questions raised for the income and expenditure account also apply to the balance sheets for the two years. For example, whether the accounts have been audited, and whether all the calculations are correct.
- Notice the way in which the total of the top part of the balance sheet is calculated. The fixed assets total (30,277.00) in year 1 is added to the

current assets less current liabilities' total (47,382.00) and the bank loan (10,000.00) is deducted to arrive at the total of 67,659.00.

- Other questions are raised on the 'working sheet' on page 95.

---

**ACCOUNTING POLICIES**

1. The accounts are prepared in accordance with the **historical cost convention** and using the **accruals accounting** basis.

2. Stock of drugs are included at the lower of cost or **net realisable value**.

3. Depreciation is calculated to write off the value of the asset over its useful life. The policy is to depreciate vehicles using the reducing balance method of depreciation at a rate of 60%. Equipment is depreciated using the straight line method of depreciation over five years.

---

**Figure 29: Lomtaka Centre's accounting policies relating to its accounts for year 2**

## KEY POINTS FROM THE ACCOUNTING POLICIES

- The historical cost convention means that the original values or cost prices have been used in the accounts. Therefore, no consideration has been taken of inflation – what was originally paid or received is what has been included. The accruals accounting basis implies that book-keeping adjustments, for example for accruals, prepayments, depreciation and bad debts have been made to the accounts.
- The term *lower of cost and net realisable value* is commonly used. It means that if the current value of the closing stock is less than its cost, the current value would be included in calculating the stock figure. This will avoid an over-valuation of any obsolete stock.
- This shows the methods and rates at which depreciation is calculated.

Accounting policies and notes are often included as part of an organisation's accounting statements. Always consult these for additional information.

## NOTES TO THE ACCOUNTS – FOR YEAR ENDING 31 DECEMBER (YEAR 2)

**Note 1:**

| Fixed Assets | Cost | Total Depreciation to Date | Net Book Value (cost *less* total dep'n) |
|---|---|---|---|
| Vehicle | 15,298 | 12,850 | 2,448 |
| Vehicles purchased, year 2 | 66,804 | 40,082 | 26,722 |
| Equipment | 30,198 | 12,080 | 18,118 |
| | 112,300 | 65,012 | 47,288 |
| **Depreciation charged (year 2)** | | | |
| Vehicle | | 6,040 | |
| Vehicles purchased | | 3,671 | |
| Equipment | | 40,082 | 49,793 |
| **Note 2:** | | | |
| Debtors | | 15,999 | |
| *Less* provision for doubtful debts | | 800 | 15,199 |
| *Plus* income in arrears | | | 20,000 |
| | | | 35,199 |
| **Note 3:** | | | |
| Creditors | | 13,513 | |
| Accruals (payments in arrears) | | 3,742 | |
| Income in advance | | 520 | 17,775 |
| **Note 4:** | | | |
| Bad debts written off | | 529 | |
| Increase in the provision for doubtful debts | | 109 | 638 |

**Figure 30: Notes to Lomtaka Centre's accounts for year 2**

## KEY POINTS FROM THE NOTES TO THE ACCOUNTS

- Notes to the accounts in this example are simply a breakdown of figures in the financial statements. Otherwise the face of the income and expenditure account and balance sheet would be cluttered with detail.
- The notes show for instance how depreciation, bad debts and a provision for doubtful debts are calculated. The balance sheet on its own does not provide all this data.

The following 'working sheets' are used to identify further questions to ask, arising from the two years' income and expenditure accounts and balance sheets.

# WORKING SHEET FOR THE TWO YEARS' INCOME AND EXPENDITURE ACCOUNTS

## QUESTIONS TO ASK

*Compare with narrative report.*

*Are additional staff or increase for existing staff in salaries figures?*

*Why 25% increase in rent?*

*Is there a connection in fees and charges and other income? If so overall decrease over 2 years?*

*Were WEV approached to increase grant? What is the background?*

*Will the Donoraid/DOH increases continue next year?*

*10.8% increase in fees and charges. Compare inflation. Will increase continue?*

*Breakdown of 'other income' needed. Why decreased?*

| Lomtaka Health Care Centre: Income and Expenditure account for the period ended 31 December (years 1 and 2) | | | |
|---|---|---|---|
| **Year 1** | | | **Year 2** |
| | **Income** | | |
| 100,000 | Grants  - WEV | | 100,000 |
| 250,000 | - Donoraid | | 300,000 |
| 350,000 | Department of Health | | 450,000 |
| 110,734 | Fees and charges | | 122,673 |
| 20,023 | Other income | | 4,537 |
| 830,757 | | | 977,210 |
| | **Expenditure** | | |
| 483,109 | Salaries | 541,748 | |
| 96,000 | Rent of premises | 120,000 | |
| 103,192 | Purchase of drugs | 126,256 | |
| 59,809 | Medical supplies | 74,768 | |
| 11,547 | Electricity | 13,486 | |
| 18,394 | Travelling expenses | 27,471 | |
| 6,778 | Training programme | 18,732 | |
| 10,887 | Office costs (including audit) | 13,791 | |
| 2,192 | Other payments | 962 | |
| 15,219 | Depreciation | 49,793 | |
| 971 | Re: Bad debts (note 4) | 638 | 987,645 |
| 808,098 | | | |
| **22,659** | **Excess of income over expenditure (Excess of expenditure over income)** | | **(10,435)** |

*Breakdown of 'other payments' and 'training' for year 2 needed.*

*Are all increases in line with inflation rate? Has programme level increased - by how much?*

*Have the accounts been audited? Fee paid but no audit report!*

*Is money set aside for replacement of assets?*

*New vehicles - should not other travel be reduced - has this happened?*

*Need tight control over expenditure.*

*'Bad debts' indicate debts reviewed methodically.*

*Increase in expenses not matched by sufficient increase in income. How will this be monitored <u>next</u> year?*

*Compare with year 2 budget.*

# WORKING SHEET FOR THE TWO YEARS' BALANCE SHEETS

## QUESTIONS TO ASK

*Fixed assets depreciated but no money set aside - how will items be replaced?*

*Slight increase in debtors. Will they all pay? How long has each debt been outstanding?*

*When is the loan repayable? What is the interest rate?*

*Relationship of current assets to current liabilities means creditors could be paid using bank and cash only.*

*Is lower stock level acceptable? Does it contain any obsolete stock?*

*Bad debts in income and expenditure indicate debtors are systematically reviewed.*

### Lomtaka Health Care Centre: Balance Sheets as at 31 December (years 1 and 2)

| Year 1 | | Year 2 |
|---|---|---|
| | **Fixed Assets** (note 1) | |
| 6,119 | Vehicles - net book value | 29,170 |
| 24,158 | Equipment - net book value | 18,118 |
| 30,277 | | 47,288 |
| | **Current Assets** | |
| 10,129 | Closing stock of drugs | 6,203 |
| 33,839 | Debtors  (note 2) | 35,199 |
| 30,385 | Bank and cash | 63,113 |
| 74,353 | | 104,515 |
| | *Less:* **Current Liabilities** | |
| (26,971) | Creditors (note 3) | (17,775) |
| 47,382 | Working capital *(current assets less current liabilities)* | 86,740 |
| | *Less:* **Long-term Liabilities** | |
| (10,000) | Bank loan | (10,000) |
| **67,659** | | **124,028** |
| | *Financed by:* | |
| | **Accumulated Fund** | |
| - | Balance brought forward | 67,659 |
| 45,000 | Capital grant - Department of Health | 66,804 |
| 22,659 | *Plus:* Excess of income over expenditure | (10,435) |
| | (Excess of expenditure over income) | |
| **67,659** | | **124,028** |

*Large increase in cash and bank - why?*

*124,028.00 represents previous years' surpluses (less deficits) plus any capital grants.*

*Deficit of 10,435.00 - OK for this year, as sufficient accumulated funds to cover it. Need to watch it does not continue next year. What action will be taken to avoid this?*

*Have accounts been audited? Where is the audit report?*

The questions highlighted in the working sheets may seem like 'common sense'! Interpretation of accounts is usually not highly technical, but rather a methodical approach to comparing figures to enable the user to see exactly what is happening. This, together with general (non-financial) knowledge, can build up a comprehensive picture of the organisation's activities.

# A STRUCTURED WAY OF ANALYSING ACCOUNTING STATEMENTS

A checklist to use when analysing accounting statements is included in Appendix A. This includes basic questions to ask. More specific questions can be added as expertise in the issues to raise is increased.

# Chapter 9

## Interpretation 'Toolkit'

---

**OBJECTIVES OF THIS CHAPTER**

There are a number of 'tools' introduced in this chapter which will help to develop the interpretation of the accounting statements. Some of these relate to the statements themselves whilst others take a more general look at the organisation.

Having considered the material in this chapter, you should be able to:

- explain the tools that can be used to interpret accounting information;
- illustrate ways that balance sheet items can be confirmed;
- calculate two liquidity ratios;
- describe other ratios which can be used to interpret statements.

---

A number of people need to interpret accounting information. The following are 'tools' which provide a practical method of using the data available.

## AUDIT REPORTS

If the organisation being examined has been audited recently, an **audit report** can be a useful tool. This is usually included at the start of the statements and expresses the auditors' opinion of the accounts.

A more detailed way of discovering the auditors' recommendations is to look at the **management letter** which is sent to an organisation at the end of its audit. This is a detailed account of issues the auditors have decided have not been fully resolved, and need further attention. It includes factual matters, the auditors' recommendations and often, the management's response. It identifies any major weaknesses which should be dealt with soon after the audit has taken place.

If the audit has been carried out by reputable auditors – particularly ones who examine *management and financial* systems as well as the figures – the management letter can be a good starting point for initiating improvements.

It is an important but sensitive document. Management and members of an NGO's governing body should have easy access to the letter. Donors may also have access to the letter if they have a good relationship with the NGO. If the report and letter are discussed in a positive way and as a means of developing institutionally, it can be a powerful tool for all concerned.

Further details about the audit process are outlined in Chapter 11.

## COMPARISON WITH BUDGET

A useful way of identifying how closely the organisation has achieved its financial objectives is to compare the income and expenditure account (or its equivalent) with the budget, as shown in the example in Chapter 8. This will identify questions to raise.

A basic rule is that the accounts should be prepared using the same headings as those included in the budget. If this is not done, it will make comparisons and questions more difficult.

It is useful to identify a level above which there needs to be an explanation for budget variances. For example, any variance above 10% (over or under budget) or a significant amount under 10% needs to be explained. Notes are particularly helpful in explaining unusual or large variances.

Identify the major questions and ask them. Be sure to be persistent!

## COMPARISON WITH PREVIOUS YEARS' ACCOUNTS

As with the budget, compare the accounting statements with previous years' statements. Often, the previous year's figures will be included with the year under review. It is useful to look back over several years to identify trends. Again, make a list of questions and ask them!

## CONFIRMING ITEMS IN THE BALANCE SHEET

The balance sheet shows the value of assets and liabilities at the end of an accounting period. The balance sheet is somewhat limited, because it is presented as at one moment in time, for example midnight on 31 December. The day after the date of the balance sheet, some of the figures will have changed.

Nonetheless, considerable analysis is possible. With several years' balance sheets, it is possible to build up an overall picture of the organisation.

It is particularly useful to assess whether the fixed and current assets shown are worth the value quoted. If the accounts have been correctly audited, the organisation should have included accurate figures, but this does not always happen.

The following are areas on which to focus.

## Fixed Assets

These are balance sheet items such as buildings, vehicles, computers, furniture and equipment. As these items lose their value, they should have been depreciated (that is some of the value is written off each year). The annual depreciation charge is included in the income and expenditure account as an expense, and the 'total depreciation charged to date' for a fixed asset and its 'net book value' are shown in the balance sheet.

Although depreciation is charged, this does not necessarily mean that there will be money available to buy new assets (see Chapter 6). A question to ask is how, for example, will a new vehicle be funded when the current one is no longer road worthy. The organisation may have to rely on outside help to achieve this.

The accounts will show the 'net book value' for an asset, but it is unlikely that this is the actual value of the asset, as depreciation is only an estimate of the loss of value. Sometimes the current market value will also be shown as a note to the accounts. It is worthwhile checking that these assets actually exist!

## Current Assets

The balance sheet list of current assets includes stock, debtors, bank balances and cash.

Bank and cash balances shown in the balance sheet are usually accurate. It is however worth asking how frequently the organisation's own bank records are reconciled with the bank statement or pass book and how often the cash is counted.

The value of any stock should reflect its saleable value. If not, the difference between this and the amount shown in the accounts can be charged as an expense in the income and expenditure account. If stock is a large figure, ask if there is any obsolete stock.

The debtors' figure should accurately reflect what is owed to the organisation. It is worth asking if all the amounts will be received and what is the 'age' of the debts. If there are individual debts of more than a year, it is unlikely that they will ever be received. The income and expenditure account may include such debts identified as 'bad debts'. If the organisation is writing off bad debts, it is examining the debtors methodically to make sure the remaining ones will pay.

## Loans

If loans are included under 'current liabilities' on the balance sheet, this suggests that they are due to be repaid within the next year. If they are included under 'long-term loans' or 'current liabilities due in more than one year', the repayment date is more than one year away. Make sure the terms and conditions of the loan are known.

Ask 'will the organisation be able to repay the loan?' If there is a surplus on the income and expenditure account, that is only a guide to its ability. There must also be enough cash. Is sufficient money being set aside to provide for the eventual repayment of the loan? The current assets, especially cash and debtors, should ideally be more than the total of the creditors and any loan repayment outstanding at the year end, to make sure that these items can be paid.

Ask whether a loan is 'hard' or 'soft'. Bank loans are sometimes described as 'hard' which means the lender is likely to insist on repayment, at whatever cost to the organisation. Loans from other NGOs or their parent body may be 'soft', indicating a more flexible approach towards repayment.

# USING RATIOS

In addition to considering the basic information within accounting statements, it is also useful to use a technique known as **ratio analysis**: expressing one figure in relation to another in an easily understandable way. Ratio analysis is a method of analysing statements to illustrate trends in the figures and as an indication of potential difficulties.

A large range of ratios can be calculated, but two categories which are useful for the interpretation of financial statements of NGOs are:

- **LIQUIDITY**
  How able is the organisation to pay its way?

- **PROGRAMME SUPPORT, FUND-RAISING AND THE PROGRAMME**
  What proportion is spent on programme support, fund-raising and the programme?

The figures for these ratios are taken from the income and expenditure account (or its equivalent) and the balance sheet.

## 1. LIQUIDITY

Liquidity refers to the money available to pay amounts that fall due. Using the extract from the Lomtaka Centre's balance sheet shown below, two important liquidity ratios can be calculated.

| | | |
|---|---:|---:|
| **Current Assets** | | |
| Closing stock of drugs | | 10,129 |
| Debtors (23,310 *less* 280) | 23,030 | |
| *Less* provision for doubtful debts | 691 | 22,339 |
| Prepayment (payment in advance) | | 1,500 |
| Income in arrears | | 10,000 |
| Bank and cash | | 30,385 |
| | | 74,353 |
| *Less:* **Current Liabilities** | | |
| Creditors | 13,236 | |
| Accruals (payments in arrears) | | |
| (8,700 + 1,485) | 10,185 | |
| Income in advance | 3,550 | 26,971 |
| *Working capital (current assets less current liabilities)* | | 47,382 |

**Figure 31: Extract from the Lomtaka Centre's balance sheet showing current assets and current liabilities**

### Current ratio

The **current ratio** identifies the relationship between current assets and current liabilities to show how able the organisation is to pay its short-term debts. If, for example, the current assets were twice as much as current liabilities, it would indicate that the organisation could easily pay its debts. However, this level of current assets to current liabilities is often not achieved. The figure needs to be interpreted in the light of the liabilities, and the type and circumstances of the organisation.

The current ratio is calculated by dividing the total of current assets by the total of current liabilities.

Using the figures from the Lomtaka Centre's balance sheet extract shown above:

$$\frac{\text{Current assets}}{\text{Current liabilities}} = \frac{74,353}{26,971} = \mathbf{2.76:1}$$

**Figure 32: Calculation of the current ratio**

Here, 2.76:1 means that the Lomtaka Centre has about two and three quarters as much in current assets as in current liabilities. This indicates that at this point in time, there is little problem in paying the creditors as these amounts fall due. Indeed, the Centre has a healthy bank balance. One question that might be asked from this is, how long the money is likely to be available (the cash budget would help to identify this) and whether the bank balance is gaining interest. There is no obvious sign of this in Lomtaka's income and expenditure account shown in Figure 20 in Chapter 6.

## Liquidity or 'Acid Test' ratio

The **liquidity ratio** is similar to the current ratio, but excludes the closing stock from the calculation, as in many organisations the stock is unlikely to be sold and turned into cash quickly. The stock held by NGOs may not be for resale. The Lomtaka Centre, for example, holds a stock of drugs; other agencies may hold stocks of printed materials. In these cases it is particularly important to exclude stock from the ratio calculated.

If the current assets, excluding stock, are about the same value as current liabilities, it indicates that the organisation could pay off its current liabilities, as long as debtors pay at about the same rate as creditors expect to be paid. The level of the liquidity ratio expected however depends on the type and circumstances of the organisation.

The calculation for the Lomtaka Centre using information from the balance sheet extract shown above, is as follows.

$$\frac{\text{Current assets (excluding stock)}}{\text{Current liabilities}} = \frac{74,353 \; less \; 10,129}{26,971} = \mathbf{2.38 : 1}$$

**Figure 33: Calculation of the liquidity ratio**

This ratio of 2.38:1 shows that the organisation has sufficient cash to pay its creditors, irrespective of the stock level. It has over twice as much in current assets (less stock) as in current liabilities.

# 2. PROGRAMME SUPPORT AND FUND-RAISING RATIOS

Other ratios commonly used in NGOs analyse how funds have been allocated between the programme objectives, programme support (or administration) and fund-raising. There is no 'correct' ratio, but it is useful to compare previous years, the budgeted figure and the ratios of similar organisations.

Programme support costs can be calculated as follows.

> Programme support  x  100
> ―――――――――――――――
> Total expenditure

**Figure 34: Calculation of programme costs as a percentage of total expenditure**

This gives the percentage of programme support costs as a proportion of total expenditure. In interpreting this, it is helpful to identify exactly what has been included in 'programme support costs'.

Fund-raising costs can usefully be compared with the funds raised, as follows.

> Costs of fund-raising  x  100
> ―――――――――――――――
> Total funds raised

**Figure 35: Calculation of fund-raising costs as a percentage of total funds raised**

This provides the percentage of fund-raising costs as a proportion of total funds raised. If different methods of fund-raising are employed, comparisons can be made as to the effectiveness of each. This can be calculated by taking the cost of a particular fund-raising method and the funds raised from it.

A figure for costs of fund-raising as a percentage of total expenditure can be found by:

> Costs of fund-raising  x  100
> ―――――――――――――――
> Total expenditure

**Figure 36: Calculation of costs of fund-raising as a percentage of total expenditure**

Where one particular type of fund-raising comprises a significant proportion of the total, it is useful to identify trends for each type over, for example, the last five years. This can highlight which particular method of fund-raising, for example donations from individuals, is providing less as a proportion of the total funds raised.

The percentage spent on an organisation's programme can be found by:

$$\frac{\text{Cost of the programme}}{\text{Total expenditure}} \quad x \quad 100$$

**Figure 37: Calculation of the cost of the programme as a percentage of total expenditure**

A breakdown of how the figure for the programme's costs have been calculated and what is included in each category is needed to interpret this ratio. Much of this information and that for the breakdown of programme support and fund-raising costs can only be found with access to an NGO's internal financial records.


## A WORD OF WARNING

Many ratios can be calculated and just a few are given here. If more are needed there are many accounting textbooks that provide a comprehensive list.

Ratios are most useful when a number of years' accounting statements are available or when the statements can be compared with a similar organisation. It is always important to ensure the figures used are comparable, that is to compare 'like with like'.

Ratios should be seen as an indication of the areas to be investigated further, rather than as giving a definitive answer.

# Chapter 10

## Internal Controls

**OBJECTIVES OF THIS CHAPTER**

The basic internal controls are examined as an introduction to the checks necessary to help prevent mistakes or possible misappropriation. Appendix B develops these rules into a checklist which can be used with an organisation.

Having considered the material in this chapter and in Appendix B, you should be able to:

- justify why sound internal controls are essential;
- describe the major internal controls;
- relate some of the controls to an organisation you know;
- explain what is meant by the 'segregation of duties';
- use the internal control checklist to identify weaknesses within a specific organisation.

It is important that financial systems are designed to make sure that as few mistakes as possible are made, and the potential for misappropriation is minimised.

A qualified accountant or auditor may be needed to ensure that good financial systems are in place, but it is essential for managers and others responsible to see that some of the basic rules are followed. These are described as **internal controls** or **financial controls** and can be defined as any action that management takes to ensure that established objectives are achieved.

The rules can be grouped into the following categories:

1. organisational structure
2. budgetary controls
3. accounting records
4. incoming funds

5. expenditure controls
6. purchase controls
7. bank accounts
8. cash transactions
9. physical controls
10. debtor controls

# 1. ORGANISATIONAL STRUCTURE

The management should have an overview of the organisation as well as of the day-to-day activities. NGOs must clearly define the allocation of responsibilities to individual staff, who should perceive the management as being effective.

There should be written policies and procedures in place to deal with financial and management issues to which all staff have access.

There must be a system to identify staff who are not performing adequately. This could be a part of an annual review of individual staff's work, their job descriptions and an identification of their training needs.

All staff must be suitably qualified for the work they do – it is essential that financial staff have the correct training and experience.

A system for identifying potential organisational problems is also needed. The process of an annual audit can provide this. The **audit report** and **management letter** should be acted upon promptly by management.

# 2. BUDGETARY CONTROLS

Budget monitoring is a key method of ensuring that the objectives of the organisation are achieved. An annual budget should be prepared and regular comparisons of the budget and actual statement (see Chapter 1) made and reviewed by senior management. Notes explaining any differences should be produced by the person responsible for the budget and attached to the budget and actual statement. Those responsible should make sure that action is taken when large differences occur.

Cash budgeting (see Chapter 2) is an excellent way of ensuring that there will be enough money available when it is needed.

# 3. ACCOUNTING RECORDS

Accurate and up-to-date accounting records should be kept, with transactions recorded as they happen. Regular summaries of the accounts in the form of budget, budget and actual reports and annual accounting statements should be presented to the **governing body**.

Accounting records will be reviewed as part of the annual audit, and action taken by staff and the governing body to follow up the auditors' recommendations.

If funding is from external donors, it is essential that the accounting system enables the donation and its related expenditure to be accounted for separately. The records should be able to provide any financial reports required by the donor.

# 4. INCOMING FUNDS

There is an element of risk in the actual receipt of all funds. Incoming mail, for example, is likely to contain cheques and should be opened in a secure place in the presence of more than one person. Cash may be received regularly and numbered receipts should be available and issued for this. Cash or cheques received should always be recorded immediately.

Internal controls can be weak when fund-raising is through public collections. Similar controls to mail opening are required, with more than one person present when money is counted. If this is a major part of the NGO's activities, further advice should be sought from a professional accountant or auditor to minimise the risk of misappropriation.

A senior person other than those responsible for incoming funds, should make regular checks to ensure that the income records are accurate.

# 5. EXPENDITURE CONTROLS

Some of the key controls for expenditure relate to *authorisation*. This ensures that there is a paperwork system, often called a **payment voucher** system, which requires a senior person to authorise expenditure *before* it is made. These vouchers can then be checked later by an auditor.

An authorisation system itself consists of one or more named staff who are given authority (possibly by the governing body) to authorise expenditure up to a certain limit. More senior staff are often given a higher level of authority.

The person authorising expenditure should be different from the one who prepares and signs the cheques. In small organisations this can be difficult, but is still required. Again the advice of a professional accountant or auditor may be needed.

A useful check against accidentally paying an amount twice is to insist that all payments to suppliers are paid only with the *original* invoice. This is a safeguard against error or when a creditor has mistakenly or deliberately sent two invoices.

# 6. PURCHASE CONTROLS

Orders for goods and services should be placed only through the official ordering system, using numbered order forms. Orders of more than a specified amount, for example the equivalent of US$200, should be subject to a formal ordering procedure where at least three quotes are obtained before an order is accepted. In some situations this may be difficult to follow, but a strict procedure ensures that there is transparency in an area where there could be potential for misappropriation.

Invoices should be matched against the original order and the quality and quantity of goods received checked on arrival. There should be a regular stocktake of goods held.

# 7. BANK ACCOUNTS

Bank accounts provide a key control of any organisation. It is essential that these rules are closely followed.

- An NGO's bank account should be registered in the name of a group or organisation – never in the name of an individual.
- Arrange with the bank that all requests for withdrawals (for example cheques) are to be signed by two named people. It is sometimes more practical to say 'any two signatories from three named individuals'. The bank should be informed that any changes in the signing arrangements can only be approved by a senior staff member, preferably one who is not a regular signatory to the account.
- If the finance officer is involved in the preparation of cheques s/he should not also be a bank signatory.
- Cheques should be written for as many payments as possible to avoid holding large amounts of cash.
- Blank cheques should never be signed. If there is no other alternative (extremely rare) make sure the name of the payee is included and a limit set on the amount payable. Some banks will allow a phrase such as 'amount not to exceed five hundred ...' to be written on the face of the cheque.

- Banks can be asked to speak with specified staff within the organisation to verify any cheques above a certain limit or that appear unusual, before they are charged to the account. This is an added safeguard to protect against fraud.
- Money received should be deposited into the bank as often as practical. This is especially important before weekends and holidays when it is unwise to leave large amounts of cash on the premises.
- Large amounts of income should be transferred directly to the bank account.
- Regular reconciliations between the bank statement and the organisation's own records should be made, each time a bank statement is received or the pass book is updated (an example of how to do this is shown in Chapter 3). This should be regularly reviewed by a senior member of the staff or the governing body.
- Cheque books should be kept in the safe or another secure place.
- The larger the number of accounts and banks the more difficult it is to ensure effective control. It is therefore advisable to hold as few accounts as possible.

# 8. CASH TRANSACTIONS

The bank should be used in preference to cash for the majority of transactions, but when cash is used the following rules should be kept.

- Cash must be held in a secure place, for example a lockable tin which is kept in a safe or locked cupboard. In many countries it is possible to obtain insurance to cover the holding of cash.
- Only one person should be responsible for the cash at any one time. When there is a change of person, both should agree the cash balance and both sign against the figure in the cash book. The person handling the cash is often known as the **cashier**.
- The cashier should, if possible, be a different person from the one dealing with other accounting records.
- All cash items received or paid should be recorded in a cash book as soon as possible after the transaction has taken place.
- Preprinted numbered receipts bearing the organisation's name, should be issued for any cash received. The top copy is given to the person paying the cash and a duplicate copy retained by the person receiving it. When money is paid out by the organisation a receipt should be requested and kept along with any other paperwork relating to the transaction.
- Large or unusual payments should be authorised by a senior person. It is

usual to set a limit beyond which the cashier should obtain written approval.

- A senior person should count the cash weekly (if possible) and agree it to the balance of cash recorded in the cash book. It is common for the person counting the cash to draw a line and initial the cash book. This avoids differences occurring and the cashier is seen to be honest.
- The cashier should monitor the amount left in the cash account and alert a senior member of staff if this becomes low.

## 9. PHYSICAL CONTROLS

Access to valuable items, for example stock, vehicles or computers should be limited to authorised staff. Complete records of items owned (an **inventory**) should be kept and updated regularly as a safeguard against theft and for accurate accounting. All items should be registered in the organisation's name rather than that of an individual.

Stores records should include entries for purchases, usage and the balance remaining, so that the physical stock can be counted and agreed.

In addition:

- All premises and stores must be kept secure.
- If possible sufficient insurance cover should be arranged for valuable items owned.
- A clear policy should be written about the use of organisational assets by staff (for example vehicles used by staff for private mileage).
- A useful check for larger organisations is to make sure that all the employees on the payroll actually exist and no extra salaries are being drawn!

## 10. DEBTOR CONTROLS

Invoices should be issued promptly for all goods or services supplied and copies retained and filed to enable reminders to be sent if the debt remains unpaid. Debts should be followed up after approximately one month of non-payment, by the member of staff responsible. It is useful to do this each month. Debts that remain unpaid after two months (or whatever time period is appropriate for the situation) should be followed up with a personal letter or telephone call.

If the debt is unpaid after three months it is worth visiting the debtor personally, and taking legal action (if the amount of the debt justifies this).

Consider not dealing with debtors who regularly delay payment. Discounts sometimes encourage prompt payment.

# SEGREGATION OF DUTIES

The **segregation of duties** is a principle affecting all areas of internal control. It aims to prevent errors and potential fraud by ensuring that one person is not responsible for the whole of any transaction. Separating the tasks, for example the authorising of a payment and signing a cheque, so that different people perform each task makes fraud more difficult.

Small organisations do not always have sufficient staff for work to be segregated adequately. In these circumstances it is necessary for someone else to be involved on a more occasional basis. For example, cash could be counted when an outside member of staff makes a random visit, or a firm of accountants or auditors (if available in the locality) could be asked to make random checks.

The fact that it is a small organisation should not provide an excuse for having inadequate internal controls. It is rather a reason to be creative about the ways of implementing them. It may be necessary to consult a qualified accountant to establish these procedures.

# PAPERWORK

It is important to control all financial stationery. Receipts, invoices and order forms, should be pre-numbered and held securely and a record of stationery used and issued should be maintained.

# DEALING WITH FRAUD

All these suggestions are designed to help prevent fraud, however sometimes there is a misappropriation of funds. This can be an extremely stressful time for the person who discovers it. If fraud is uncovered or suspected, it is important not to panic but to call on professional accounting and legal advice, and on friends to give moral support. An extra audit may be needed and it may be necessary to involve the police. It is important to make sure that any evidence, for example cash books and receipt books, is not destroyed by the person committing the fraud.

# A STRUCTURED WAY OF ASSESSING INTERNAL CONTROLS

Appendix B contains a checklist that can be used to assess an organisation in relation to the basic principles of internal control.

# Chapter 11

## Audit of the Accounts

---

**OBJECTIVES OF THIS CHAPTER**

This chapter outlines the auditing process: what it is and what an organisation can expect from an audit.

Having considered the material in this chapter, you should be able to:

- describe the stages of appointing an auditor;
- explain what is meant by the terms 'audit report' and 'management letter';
- summarise the differences between a 'financial' and 'management' audit;
- distinguish between an 'internal' and 'external' audit;
- relate the value of an audit to an NGO.

---

An **audit** is an independent review of an organisation's accounting, financial and management processes. The audit of accounts may be required by law, but whether or not this is the case, it is a worthwhile investment. It can give an objective view of financial and management processes, and can increase an NGO's effectiveness.

## APPOINTMENT OF THE AUDITOR

Auditors are usually from a firm of professional accountants. It is possible to employ an auditor from a large international firm or from a smaller local firm. In order to decide which auditor to use, it is advisable to talk with the person who will actually be undertaking the work, and to ask other similar organisations or a local government office or embassy for their experience of using different firms of auditors.

Many NGOs will invite a number of auditing firms, often three, to **tender** for the work. This is an opportunity to identify exactly what will be covered in their audit and to clarify specific points. It is worth going into detail at this stage to prevent misunderstandings occurring later.

Compare the costs and the level of service included in the tenders. The overall cost of an audit should be included in the budget. Some donors are willing to fund this as part of their support for an NGO.

It is good practice to change auditors occasionally or to change the auditor within the same firm. This ensures the relationship between the NGO and the auditor is an impartial one.

Sometimes an **honorary auditor** who may be unpaid, is appointed. If the person has the relevant skills, and most importantly is *independent*, this can work well. In many countries there are strict legal guidelines stating who can act as auditor, often linked to the size of the organisation.

# LETTER OF ENGAGEMENT

It is common for an agreement to be signed between the auditor and the organisation, stating the scope of the audit and the fee payable. The size of the fee does not always relate to the quality of the audit! The agreement or **letter of engagement** should be in writing.

# THE AUDIT ITSELF

A good audit starts with the auditor obtaining a comprehensive understanding of the organisation. Auditors will want to examine accounting and other records, sometimes following a standard programme for their work. They will expect to have access to any documents or records they wish to see. In the interests of transparency, it is wise to encourage this. The audit will usually include a check of the figures in the accounts and an examination of the financial and management systems.

The audit may take place in more than one stage. The auditors will want to spend time with the NGO (if it is anything other than a small group) immediately after the end of the financial year. This process can take several weeks in a complex organisation. If there is a great deal of work involved, the auditors may carry out an **interim audit** during the year to help them manage their heavier workload at the end of a financial year.

# AFTER THE AUDIT

When the audit is almost completed, the auditor will list issues that have not been fully resolved during the audit. The auditor will ask the management of the organisation to respond. This process should help to clarify many of the outstanding issues.

At the end of the audit a draft **management letter** is written by the auditors to the management. The NGO may clarify particular points raised, and these points will not be included in subsequent drafts of the letter. The final version of the management letter may also include comments by the management on each of the issues raised.

The management letter is an extremely useful document that identifies what is needed to reach the required standard and is a valuable part in an organisation's development. The NGO governing body will want to discuss this fully, and may want to share the letter with its donors. This enables both parties to consider ways in which improvements could be made. The management letter might contain sensitive information, and the level to which it is shared will depend on the relationship of those concerned. Some donors however request that this document is made available to them each year.

The auditors should always prepare a management letter. The letter however tends by its nature to select the negative rather than the positive points and the reader needs to be aware of this.

---

1. A number of advances were outstanding for staff that were not fully accounted for at 31 December (year 1). A more comprehensive system of financial control is required to ensure that these are followed up.

Management comment on paragraph 1
These advances have subsequently been accounted for in full. A new advances register has been introduced to ensure no new advances will be issued until accounts are provided for any outstanding ones.

2. Payment vouchers and connected documents have not been stamped to state they have been paid. All of these should be so stamped and dated to avoid the possible reuse of a document.

Management comment on paragraph 2
The office has not held a 'paid' stamp. However, one has now been purchased and a system introduced to make sure that all documents are stamped.

---

> 3. Grant income received from international donors has not always been spent in the way specified by the donor. The Centre's accounting records do not show income which has been given for a particular purpose identified separately.
>
> Management comment on paragraph 3
> We accept the auditors' observation that the accounting records do not separately identify all income received for a particular purpose. A new accounting procedure has been introduced which will rectify this.
>
> We do not however accept that grant income received was not used for the purpose given. We understood that this income was unrestricted and as such used towards the general running costs of the Centre.

**Figure 38: Extract from the management letter received by the Lomtaka Centre**

Some system of follow-up is necessary to ensure that the recommendations contained in the management letter are implemented.

## THE AUDIT REPORT

An **audit report** will be prepared and attached to the accounting statements when circulated. This will include standard comments, the topics of which are often required by law. In addition, any unusual or unresolved points raised in the management letter may be included if they affect the statements. In some countries the report on a small NGO may include a paragraph referring to the limitation of financial controls caused by the relatively small number of staff.

The audit report gives the **auditors' opinion** on the accounting records and financial statements of an organisation. This opinion – usually the final paragraph of the auditors' report – often states that the accounts show a 'true and fair view' of the organisation's activities. A positive (or **unqualified**) opinion however may be expressed using other words. If anything else is included (a **qualified audit report**) it is likely to be a point that could not be resolved between the auditors and the organisation's management, and is therefore a serious issue.

At the end of the audit the accounts are **signed off** which means that the auditors will sign the audit report and a representative of the organisation, the accounts. This indicates that the audit is complete.

We have audited the accounting records of the Lomtaka Health Care Centre, together with the financial statements for the year ended 31 December (year 1) set out on pages 4–8. These have been prepared in accordance with the accounting policies shown in the notes to the accounts. The audit was conducted in accordance with generally accepted auditing standards.

As with many similar organisations of this size, the procedures of internal control rely on the close involvement of the Centre's management. We have accepted the assurance of the Centre's management that there has been appropriate authorisation and incurring of expenditure for the benefit of the Centre. Funds raised as a result of voluntary donations cannot be verified until they appear in the Centre's accounting records.

The financial statements have been prepared in accordance with National Accounting Standards. In our opinion the accounts present a true and fair view of the state of the Lomtaka Health Care Centre's affairs for the year ended 31 December (year 1).

..........................................
Auditors

Date: .............................

**Figure 39: Example of an audit report for the Lomtaka Centre with no additional comments (unqualified audit report)**

We have audited the accounting records of the Lomtaka Health Care Centre, together with the financial statements for the year ended 31 December (year 1) set out on pages 4–8. These have been prepared in accordance with the accounting policies shown in the notes to the accounts. The audit was conducted in accordance with generally accepted auditing standards.

As with many similar organisations of this size, the procedures of internal control rely on the close involvement of the Centre's management. We have accepted the assurance of the Centre's management that there has been appropriate authorisation and incurring of expenditure for the benefit of the Centre. Funds raised as a result of voluntary donations cannot be verified until they appear in the Centre's accounting records.

Whilst conducting the audit, we have found examples of grant income received which has not, in our opinion, been used for the purpose for which it was given. These items were not accounted for in a way we would normally expect of an organisation of this type.

The financial statements have been prepared in accordance with National Accounting Standards. Except for the comment in the last paragraph, in our opinion the accounts present a true and fair view of the state of the Lomtaka Health Care Centre's affairs for the year ended 31 December (year 1).

...................................
Auditors

Date: ...........................

**Figure 40: Example of an audit report for the Lomtaka Centre with a negative additional comment in paragraph 3 (qualified audit report)**

# FINANCIAL AND MANAGEMENT AUDITS

A **financial audit** examines the accounting records and statements of the organisation together with financial systems. A **management audit** looks more broadly at the whole organisation, its management system and the effectiveness of its work.

Ideally both are undertaken and many firms automatically do both. However, this cannot be assumed and it is sensible to ask the auditors precisely what they will do before engaging them, and to make sure that the details are included in the letter of engagement.

# INTERNAL AND EXTERNAL AUDITS

The process described above refers to an **external audit**, where the auditor is appointed from outside the organisation. Larger organisations may also employ their own auditors who conduct an **internal audit**. The work of both types of auditor is similar, but internal auditors often concentrate on internal financial systems, rather than the detail of the annual accounting statements. Both types of audit may take place within the same organisation.

Donors sometimes employ their own internal auditors to confirm that their funds have been properly accounted for, but a full external audit will often also be needed. An NGO should welcome both types of auditors!

# WHY AN AUDIT IS NECESSARY

Even if an audit is not required by law, it can provide essential information to improve the management and effectiveness of an NGO. In addition, if the accounts have been externally audited, it confirms to donors that the organisation has reached a certain level of accountability. When the organisation is willing to share its management letter with donors, it shows transparency and an excellent relationship of trust.

# Appendix A

## Checklist for Analysing Accounting Statements

### THE BUDGET

*'A financial plan relating to a period of time'*

1. When was the budget produced? If produced after the year in question has commenced it will be of less use in controlling income and expenditure.

2. How do the figures compare with the previous year's actuals (shown in the income and expenditure account) and with the previous year's budget? Ask questions about major increases or decreases.

3. How realistic is the budget? Have any unrealistic assumptions been made for income or expenditure items, for example income from fees and charges? Is the organisation likely to be able to keep within its budget?

4. Does the annual budget reflect current goals and objectives?

5. Will all grants be received in full on the due dates?

6. What is the estimated rate of inflation? How close is this to the actual increases recorded in last year's accounts? How realistic is the rate?

7. What exchange rate (if any) has been used?

8. Have all items of expenditure been included? Are they all justified?

9. Has/should depreciation be included in the budget?

10. Is an audit fee included?

11. Are there any unjustified 'miscellaneous', 'contingency' or 'other' items?

12. Is there an income budget? What proportion of the funds necessary have been secured? What is the status of any grants already requested? Have other donors been approached for funding?

13. Are the calculations correct?

14. Has a cash budget (cash flow forecast) been prepared to forecast when money will be received and paid? Are there are any months when the organisation will have insufficient or excess money? What will be done about this?

15. Will the accounting system be able to produce the accounting information in the same format as the budget? Will it produce data in the format required by donors?

## BUDGET AND ACTUAL STATEMENT

Also known as a Financial Report, Variance Report and by many other names.

*'A statement produced regularly comparing budgeted and actual income and expenditure'*

1. Have the 'actual' figures been adjusted for **accruals** and **prepayments**? If they have, it is safe to compare the figures.

2. How well is the organisation achieving its stated objectives? (A narrative report will be needed in addition to this statement.)

3. How recent is the period being examined? If examining statements for a period which ended several months ago, there may be little action that is now relevant for the current financial year.

4. Is anyone responsible for monitoring the budget and actual statement? Has any action already been taken as a result of this statement? If no one within an NGO has this responsibility, a donor agency may wish personally to examine the statements in detail.

5. Are notes attached to the statement to explain major variances and any action taken?

6. How up to date is the accounting system? If not, some actual figures may have been estimated (for comparison purposes), thus the information *may* be less accurate.

7. Has the budget been divided by twelve for a month-to-month comparison, or have the figures for income and expenditure been allocated to the month in which they will be received or paid.

8. Compare the budget and actual amounts item by item. Identify the reason for differences which are over or under budget by more than 10%. Examine smaller, but still significant, differences.

9. Actual salaries should be reasonably close to the budgeted figure. If not, why is this?

10. Are the calculations correct?

11. What would happen if the present pattern of income and expenditure were to continue for the rest of the year?

12. Is the presentation of the statement adequate to provide managers with clear data for decision-making? Does the grouping of budget items reflect the organisational structure and management?

## RECEIPTS AND PAYMENTS ACCOUNT

*'A summary of cash and bank transactions'*

1. Have the accounts been audited and if so, by whom? If not, the figures can be confirmed by examining the cash book and other accounting records.

2. Compare each of the figures with (if available):

   - the previous year's financial statements;
   - the budget for the same year as the accounts;
   - the budget for the following year.

A receipts and payments account may not however be comparing 'like with like'.

3.  Identify the reasons for any changes, or ask questions to clarify this.

4.  Use your knowledge of the organisation to assess how appropriate is each item of expenditure.

5.  If one figure contains several items grouped together (or you suspect it may do), obtain a breakdown of particular amounts to give more detail. Beware of large 'miscellaneous', 'contingency' or 'other' figures.

6.  If you are a donor, do the grants received by the organisation cross-check with your own records?

7.  Has every grant intended for a specific purpose been so applied? Ensure no items have been funded more than once, for example by another donor.

8.  Are the calculations correct?

9.  Are any other cash or bank accounts owned by the organisation?

10. What is owned by the organisation on a long-term basis? (For example, vehicles, computers, machinery, equipment, furniture.) Are these items appropriate? Has any money been set aside for the eventual replacement of these items in, for example, a bank savings account?

**Note:** One receipts and payments account will not show all the items owned (unless a balance sheet has also been prepared or it is the first year of activity). Go back over several years' receipts and payments accounts and list the larger long-term items purchased, for example vehicles, computers, furniture. Unless an item has now been sold (an entry in the receipts side of the account would show money from the sale), check to see the items still exist.

## INCOME AND EXPENDITURE ACCOUNT

Also called a Revenue Account, Operating Statement, Income and Expenditure Statement or Income Statement. A Profit and Loss Account or a Trading and Profit and Loss Account is the equivalent for an income-generating or commercial organisation.

*'A statement of what has actually been received and paid, adjusted for any items that <u>should</u> have been received or paid, and items that relate to the period of the account' – this includes adjustments for items owed and paid in advance, depreciation and bad debts. The account excludes purchase and sale of 'fixed assets' such as buildings, vehicles and equipment.*

1.  Have the accounts been audited and if so, by whom? If not, the figures can be confirmed by examining the cash book and other accounting records. It is also worth looking through the ledger (if there is one).

2.  Compare each of the figures with (if available):

    * the previous year's financial statements;
    * the budget for the same year as the accounts;
    * the budget for the following year.

3.  Identify the reasons for any changes between the figures for items in two years' income and expenditure accounts. Also, between the current budget and the income and expenditure account figure, or between the income and expenditure account figure and the following year's budget. Ask questions to clarify any unusual changes.

4.  Use your knowledge of the organisation to assess how appropriate is each item of expenditure.

5.  If one figure contains several items grouped together (or you suspect it may do), obtain a breakdown of particular amounts to give more detail. Beware of large 'miscellaneous', 'contingency' or 'other' figures.

6.  If you are a donor, do the grants received by the organisation agree with your own records?

7.  Has every grant intended for a specific purpose been so applied? Make sure no items have been funded more than once, for example by another donor.

8.  Are the calculations correct?

9.  Has depreciation been included *and* has money been set aside to pay for the replacement of large items, for example vehicles, equipment, computers?

10. Have any 'bad debts' been charged against income? If so, this indicates that a systematic review of outstanding debts has taken place to identify any debts unlikely to be received. If bad debts are not so charged, ask how often the debtors' figures are reviewed.

11. Has this account achieved a surplus (an excess of income over expenditure) or a deficit (an excess of expenditure over income)? If a deficit, how will this be changed into a surplus in future years?

## BALANCE SHEET

Also called Statement of Assets and Liabilities, Position Statement, Statement of Affairs.

A balance sheet would usually be presented with an income and expenditure account or its equivalent.

*'A photograph of what an organisation owes and owns at a single point in time'*

1. Have the accounts been audited?

2. What items have changed since the previous balance sheet? Notes to the balance sheet will often give details of this.

3. Is the current asset of stock all saleable? Is there any obsolete stock?

4. Will outstanding debtors all pay? Should any items be treated as 'bad debts'?

5. Are there any outstanding advances (for example to staff) included in the balance sheet? How long have they been outstanding? When will the amount be repaid or accounted for?

6. Is any money invested (shown as a long-term or current asset)? What interest is gained on this? How secure is the investment? How accessible is it?

7. Do the current liabilities include all amounts owed by the organisation in the short term? If the accounts have been audited, the answer can be assumed to be yes.

8. How does the total amount of current assets compare with the total of current liabilities? Ideally, current assets should be at least as much as current liabilities (preferably more) if the organisation is able to meet all its short-term commitments. Current assets may be less if, for example, a large amount of income is due at the beginning of the next financial period. The relationship between current assets and current liabilities can vary considerably, depending on the type and circumstances of the organisation under review.

9. Do the external liabilities (that is excluding the accumulated fund or capital) exceed total fixed and current assets? If so, the organisation is unable to pay its debts (technically described as **insolvent**), and any new grants allocated will be used only to settle previous debts.

10. How secure is the financial structure? It should not be necessary, for example, for an organisation to sell a fixed asset to pay its creditors.

11. Is any deficit in the current year covered by previous years' surpluses? Previous years' surpluses are part of the accumulated fund or its equivalent. If there is a deficit, how will a similar situation be avoided next year?

# Appendix B

## Internal Control Checklist

---

**GENERAL INFORMATION**

Name of group or organisation .................................................................

Name of person interviewed ...................................................................

Name of person interviewing...................................................................

Date of interview...................................................................................

**FINANCIAL DATA**

Amount of annual budget .......................................................................

Sources of funding .................................................................................

Number and names of bank account .......................................................

Name of auditors and contact person ......................................................

| QUESTION | ANSWER | COMMENTS |
|---|---|---|
| **1. ORGANISATIONAL STRUCTURE**<br><br>1.1 Is there a plan which allocates responsibilities to individual staff? | | |
| 1.2 Is the delegation of authority and responsibility clearly defined? | | |
| 1.3 Are policies and procedures written down and are all staff aware of these? | | |
| 1.4 Are the staff responsible for the finance department suitably qualified? What is the level of qualification? | | |
| 1.5 Is there an adequate segregation of financial duties? | | |
| 1.6 Are all staff trained adequately? | | |
| 1.7 Is there a staff appraisal system? | | |
| 1.8 Does management review operations, as well as the day-to-day activities? | | |

| QUESTION | ANSWER | COMMENTS |
|---|---|---|
| **2.   BUDGETARY CONTROLS** | | |
| 2.1  Is an annual budget prepared for the whole organisation? | | |
| 2.2  Is actual expenditure and income measured against the budget at regular intervals? At what interval? Who reviews this? | | |
| 2.3  Are explanations noted for significant variances? | | |
| 2.4  Is a cash budget (cash flow forecast) prepared and regularly updated? Has the organisation ever run out of money? | | |
| **3.   ACCOUNTING RECORDS** | | |
| 3.1  Are the following accounting records accurate and up to date: | | |
| • Cash book (cash and bank) Date of last entry? | | |
| • Expenditure receipts/invoices | | |
| • Income receipts | | |
| • Bank statements Date of last statement? | | |
| • Bank reconciliation Date of last reconciliation? | | |

| QUESTION | ANSWER | COMMENTS |
|---|---|---|
| **Petty cash (if additional)**<br><br>• Petty cash book<br>  Date of last entry?<br><br>• Payment vouchers<br><br>• Expenditure receipts/invoices<br><br>• Petty cash reconciliation<br>  Date of last reconciliation? | | |
| **Other records**<br><br>• Ledger (if appropriate)<br><br>• Salaries and wages records<br><br>• Records of staff advances/floats<br>  Any outstanding? | | |
| 3.2 Is the governing body presented with summaries of accounting information? Date when last presented? | | |
| 3.3 Are annual accounting statements prepared? | | |
| 3.4 Are the statements subject to an external audit? Date of last audit? | | |
| 3.5 Are audit recommendations implemented? How is this achieved? | | |
| 3.6 Is financial data used for planning purposes? | | |

| QUESTION | ANSWER | COMMENTS |
|---|---|---|
| 3.7 Do the accounting records clearly identify funds given for a specific purpose? How? | | |
| 3.8 Is sufficient information available to report back to each donor in the way requested? Have such reports been produced for the last accounting period? | | |
| **4. INCOMING FUNDS** | | |
| 4.1 Is incoming mail opened in the presence of more than one member of staff? | | |
| 4.2 Are all incoming cash and cheques entered in the cash book immediately and banked regularly? Date of last entries? | | |
| 4.3 Are acknowledgements issued to donors upon receipt of funds? | | |
| 4.4 Is unopened mail secure? | | |
| 4.5 Are regular checks made by someone other than the person originally recording the funds, to ensure income records are accurate? Date of last check? | | |
| 4.6 Are there any income-generating activities? | | |
| 4.7 If the answer to 4.6 is yes, briefly describe the control system. | | |

| QUESTION | ANSWER | COMMENTS |
|---|---|---|
| **5. EXPENDITURE CONTROLS**<br><br>5.1 Is all expenditure authorised by a senior member of staff? Who are authorising staff? | | |
| 5.2 Are appropriate (financial) limits placed on the amount staff are able to authorise? What are these limits? | | |
| 5.3 Do different staff authorise payments to those who prepare and sign cheques? | | |
| 5.4 Are payments made only with an original invoice? | | |
| **6. PURCHASE CONTROLS**<br><br>6.1 Is there an adequate system for procurement? Are several quotes obtained? Who is responsible? | | |
| 6.2 Are invoices matched against orders? | | |
| 6.3 Is the quality and quantity of goods received checked? By whom? | | |
| 6.4 Is there a regular stock-take of goods? Date of last stock-take? | | |
| **7. BANK ACCOUNTS**<br><br>7.1 Are all accounts registered in the name of the group or organisation? | | |
| 7.2 Are there at least two signatories responsible for signing cheques on each bank account? Names of signatories? | | |

| QUESTION | ANSWER | COMMENTS |
|---|---|---|
| 7.3  Are blank cheques ever pre-signed? If yes, how can this be avoided? | | |
| 7.4  Are all bank transactions recorded in the cash book immediately? | | |
| 7.5  Are cheques written for as many payments as possible? | | |
| 7.6  Are cheque-books kept in a secure place? | | |
| 7.7  Are bank accounts reconciled each time a statement is received or at least monthly? Date of last reconciliation? | | |
| 7.8  What happens to cancelled cheques? | | |
| **8.  CASH TRANSACTIONS** 8.1  Is cash kept securely? Who holds the keys? | | |
| 8.2  Are all transactions recorded in the cash book immediately? Date of last entry? | | |
| 8.3  Is a numbered receipt issued for cash received? | | |
| 8.4  Does someone other than the cashier authorise large or unusual payments? Name of person? | | |
| 8.5  Does the cashier monitor the cash balance? | | |

| QUESTION | ANSWER | COMMENTS |
|---|---|---|
| 8.6 Is the cash counted regularly by a senior member of staff, in the cashier's presence? Date cash last counted? | | |
| **9.  PHYSICAL CONTROLS** 9.1 Is there a record of all fixed assets owned? | | |
| 9.2 Is this record updated regularly? Date of last entry? | | |
| 9.3 Is the insurance cover sufficient for the current value of the items owned? (if insurance is available) | | |
| 9.4 Do all the fixed assets shown in the accounts, actually exist? How are items controlled that are no longer needed? | | |
| 9.5 How will items owned be replaced when they wear out? (Is there a savings fund?) | | |
| 9.6 Are all items owned kept securely? | | |
| 9.7 Is entry to the premises secure? | | |
| 9.8 Are any vehicles used for private mileage? Is there a log book? Is the value refunded? | | |
| 9.9 Are staff charged for the personal use of telephones? | | |
| 9.10 Is all financial stationery (for example receipt books, order forms) numbered, named and held securely? | | |

| QUESTION | ANSWER | COMMENTS |
|---|---|---|
| 9.11 How are salary payments made? Who authorises the payroll? | | |
| 9.12 Do all employees on the payroll, actually exist? | | |
| **10. DEBTOR CONTROLS** <br> 10.1 Are invoices issued promptly? | | |
| 10.2 Are unpaid invoices followed up? Length of time before this happens? | | |
| 10.3 Is the outstanding debtors' figure regularly reviewed? | | |
| **11. OTHER AREAS NOT INCLUDED ABOVE** | | |
| | | |
| | | |
| | | |
| | | |
| | | |
| | | |
| | | |
| | | |
| | | |

**12. <u>ACTION POINTS</u>**

DATE OF REVIEW OF ACTION POINTS ...............................................................

Signed    ...................................................... (Job title.............................................)

          ...................................................... (Job title.............................................)

Date      ........................................................

## NOTES ON THE USE OF THE INTERNAL CONTROL CHECKLIST

This checklist is designed for use by either financial or non-financial staff. It can be used within any organisation to assess the effectiveness of the financial controls. Ideally a senior member of the organisation should answer the questions but it may be necessary to involve finance and other staff to help answer some of the questions.

Additional questions may be added to customise the checklist to a particular organisation, or to a part of an organisation. An essential step, as a result of its use, is to write a list of *action points* (section 12 of the checklist) to be taken jointly between the parties involved. If more than one person is involved, it gives an added incentive to ensure that the points are followed up.

When used in an organisation other than the compiler's own, a non-financial facilitator is often more appropriate and less threatening. ***Whenever the checklist is used in this way it should be as a means of trying to improve the financial and management capacity of the organisation.***

Further information about the topics of the questions can be found in Chapter 10 'Internal Controls'.

# Appendix C

## International Variations in Terminology and Format

**TERMINOLOGY**

*ALTERNATIVE TERMS*

1. **INCOME AND EXPENDITURE ACCOUNT**
   **(The commercial equivalent to this account is the Trading and Profit and Loss account)**

   Revenue account or statement
   Operating statement
   Income and expenditure statement
   Statement of income and expenditure
   Income statement
   Income and disbursements account
   Statement of earnings
   Account of operations

**TERMS USED WITHIN THE INCOME AND EXPENDITURE ACCOUNT, THE PROFIT AND LOSS ACCOUNT AND THE RECEIPTS AND PAYMENTS ACCOUNT**

| | |
|---|---|
| Income | Revenue |
| Expenditure | Expenses |
| Local travel | Conveyance |
| Office administration | Establishment costs |
| Pension fund | Provident fund (especially Asia) |
| Caution money | Deposit |
| Depreciation | Value reduction |
| Employment tax (National Insurance, Social Security) | Social insurance/professional tax |

| TERMINOLOGY | ALTERNATIVE TERMS |
|---|---|
| Muslim tax to government (usually not applicable to people of other faiths) | 'Zakht' (Arabic countries) |
| Sales (in trading accounts) | Turnover or revenue |
| Net profit (profit and loss accounts) | Net margin |
| Excess of income over expenditure | Surplus (possibly profit) |
| Excess of expenditure over income | Deficit (possibly loss) |

## 2. BALANCE SHEET

Statement of assets and liabilities
Statement of financial position
Statement of condition
Position statement
Statement of affairs

## TERMS USED IN THE BALANCE SHEET

**Fixed Assets**
Land and buildings
Furniture, computers etc.

**Long-lived/Permanent Assets**
Immobile assets
Mobile assets

**Current Assets**

Stock
Debtors (those who owe money)

**Short-lived Assets/Circulating Assets/Floating Assets**
Inventory or inventories
Receivables or accounts receivable (especially in North and South America)

Payments in advance
Prepayments

**Current Liabilities**
Creditors (those to whom money is owed)

Payables or accounts payable (especially North and South America)

Payments in arrears
Accruals

| TERMINOLOGY | ALTERNATIVE TERMS |
|---|---|
| **Long-Term Liabilities** | |
| Endowment fund (employees savings scheme) | Thrift fund |
| | |
| **Accumulated Fund** | Capital (the value of initial funds plus surpluses and less deficits) (Capital is more usual for profit-making organisations) Capital fund or capital employed Funds or funds employed Project funds Reserves or retained earnings (Reserves maybe instead of other terms or in addition to them) Special funds/designated funds/ special reserves (May be part of accumulated fund – identified for a particular purpose) Membership fees/contributions (terms often used with co-operatives) |

**These are some common accounting terms used internationally. Add to them as you find others!**

# INTERNATIONAL EXAMPLES

These four examples give an idea of the range of different accounting presentations that exist. There are others. Even within countries, there can be variations in presentation. However, when confident with the information contained in the statements, the presentation becomes less of an obstacle to interpreting what the statements show.

The examples of the receipts and payments account, income and expenditure account and balance sheet use the Lomtaka Centre information shown in Figures 20 and 21 in Chapter 6. Try to interpret these statements as you go through. The results of this analysis should be the same as shown in Chapter 8.

140

## EXAMPLE 1

This example is a common presentation in Asia. It shows the equivalent receipts and payments account for the Lomtaka Centre shown in Figure 11 in Chapter 3, in addition to a format of the income and expenditure account and balance sheet.
   Note the following differences in presentation.

- The words 'to' for each item of receipt/income and 'by' for each item of payment/expenditure are used. (An old-fashioned convention, now largely ignored.)
- Some of the figures are broken down with more detail (for example 'other income' and 'other expenditure'). If comparing this with the budget, a similar breakdown of the estimated figures is required.
- Income and expenditure is side by side: expenditure on the left, income on the right. Some presentations show this in a similar way, but have the income on the left.
- The two halves of the balance sheet are shown side by side.
- The capital gift is shown separately to the capital fund.
- Current assets and current liabilities are shown separately.
- The name of the bank is given.
- An extra comma is included to signify a lakh – that is one hundred thousand.

| Lomtaka Health Care Centre: Receipts and Payments account for the period ended 31 December (year 1) | | | |
|---|---|---|---|
| RECEIPTS | AMOUNT | PAYMENTS | AMOUNT |
| To Cash in Grameen Bank | 0 | By Salaries | 4,83,109 |
| To Grant-in-aid | 6,90,000 | By Rent of premises | 96,000 |
| To Fees and charges | 90,974 | By Purchase of drugs | 95,900 |
| To Other income | 20,023 | By Medical supplies | 56,794 |
| To Department of Health | 45,000 | By Electricity | 11,547 |
| To Bank loan | 10,000 | By Travelling expenses | 18,394 |
| | | By Training programme | 5,293 |
| | | By Office costs (including audit) | 10,887 |
| | | By Other payments | 2,192 |
| | | By Purchase of vehicle | 15,298 |
| | | By Purchase of equipment | 30,198 |
| | | By Cash in Grameen Bank | 30,385 |
| | 8,55,997 | | 8,55,997 |

**Lomtaka Health Care Centre: Income and Expenditure account for the period ended 31 December (year 1)**

| EXPENDITURE | AMOUNT | INCOME | AMOUNT |
|---|---|---|---|
| To Salaries | 4,83,109 | By Grant received from | |
| " Rent of premises | 96,000 |    WEV | 1,00,000 |
| " Purchase of drugs | 1,03,192 | " Grant received from | |
| " Medical supplies | 59,809 |    Donoraid | 2,50,000 |
| " Electricity | 11,547 | " Department of Health | 3,50,000 |
| " Travelling expenses | 18,394 | " Fees and charges | 1,10,734 |
| " Training programme | 6,778 | " Interest | 1,395 |
| " Telephone | 4,895 | " Donations | 15,302 |
| " Stationery | 3,392 | " Sale of waste paper | 690 |
| " Audit | 2,600 | " Miscellaneous | 2,636 |
| " Entertainment | 204 | | |
| " Postage | 639 | | |
| " Miscellaneous | 1,349 | | |
| " Depreciation | | | |
|   - equipment | 6,040 | | |
|   - vehicle | 9,179 | | |
| " Bad debts written off | 280 | | |
| " Provision for doubtful debts | 691 | | |
| Excess of Income over Expenditure transferred to the Balance Sheet | 22,659 | | |
| TOTAL | 8,30,757 | TOTAL | 8,30,757 |

**Lomtaka Health Care Centre: Balance Sheet as at 31 December (year 1)**

| CAPITAL AND LIABILITIES | AMOUNT | PROPERTY AND ASSETS | | AMOUNT |
|---|---|---|---|---|
| Capital gift (capitalised) | 45,000 | VEHICLE | | |
| | | Cost price | 15,298 | |
| CAPITAL FUND | | less depreciation | 9,179 | 6,119 |
| Excess of Income over | | EQUIPMENT | | |
| Expenditure during year | 22,659 | Cost price | 30,198 | |
| | | less depreciation | 6,040 | 24,158 |
| LOANS | | | | |
| Grameen Bank | 10,000 | STOCK | | |
| | | Opening balance | 0 | |
| CURRENT LIABILITIES | | New stock | 10,129 | 10,129 |
| Creditors etc. | 26,971 | DEBTORS, ETC. | | 33,839 |
| | | | | |
| | | CASH IN HAND | 824 | |
| | | CASH AT BANK | 29,561 | 30,385 |
| TOTAL | 1,04,630 | | TOTAL | 1,04,630 |

## EXAMPLE 2

This example is based on an original format produced by an international firm of accountants based in Africa. This style is also used in other parts of the world.

Note the following differences in presentation.

- The account title: Income and Expenditure *Statement*.
- Details of individual grants are not included. A breakdown will need to be requested as the notes do not cover this.
- The expenditure is separated into categories – this may be helpful for managing the programme.
- The 'undocumented expenses' need further explanation.
- The total of each section is added together to give the total expenditure figure of 808,098.
- The notes to the accounts give further explanations – a valuable addition.
- Different descriptions in the balance sheet.

## Lomtaka Health Care Centre
## INCOME AND EXPENDITURE STATEMENT
## for the period ended 31 December (year 1)

|  | Note | Year 1 |
|---|---|---|
| **INCOME** | | |
| Grants | | 700,000 |
| Fees | | 110,734 |
| Other income | | 20,023 |
| | | **830,757** |
| **EXPENDITURE** | | |
| **Operating Costs** | | |
| Depreciation | 1 | 15,219 |
| Bad debts | 2 | 971 |
| Office costs | | 10,887 |
| Electricity | | 11,547 |
| Rent of premises | | 96,000 |
| Undocumented expenses | | 2,192 |
| | | 136,816 |
| **Health materials** | | |
| Purchase of drugs | 3 | 103,192 |
| Medical supplies | | 59,809 |
| | | 163,001 |
| **Vehicle/travel costs** | | |
| Travelling expenses | | 18,394 |
| | | 18,394 |
| **Staffing costs** | | |
| Salaries | | 483,109 |
| Training programme | | 6,778 |
| | | 489,887 |
| **Total expenditure** | | **808,098** |
| Surplus for the year | | **22,659** |

---

**Lomtaka Health Care Centre**
**BALANCE SHEET AT 31 DECEMBER (YEAR 1)**
Note

**FUNDS EMPLOYED**
**Project fund**    4    67,659

**Loans**    10,000

   **77,659**

**EMPLOYMENT OF FUNDS**
**Fixed Assets**    1    30,277

**Current Assets**
Closing stock    10,129
Accounts receivable    22,339
Prepayments etc.    11,500
Cash in hand and at bank    30,385
   74,353

**Current Liabilities**
Accounts payable    (13,236)
Accruals etc.    (13,735)
   (26,971)

**Net Current Assets**    47,382
   **77,659**

---

Note 1: Depreciation has been charged using the reducing balance method for vehicles and the straight line method for all other items.

| | Vehicle | | Equipment | |
|---|---|---|---|---|
| Cost | 15,298 | Cost | | 30,198 |
| Depreciation | 9,179 | Depreciation | | 6,040 |
| Net book value | 6,119 | Net book value | | 24,158 |

Note 2: Bad debts have been written off at the end of the year and a provision of 3% has been made, based on the accounts receivable at the end of the year.

Note 3: The stock of drugs at the end of the year had a value of 10,129.00. The purchase of drugs shown in the income and expenditure statement is net of this figure.

Note 4: Project funds were made up as follows:
Capital grant – Department of Health    45,000
*Plus* surplus for the year    22,659
   67,659

## EXAMPLE 3

The following example is based on a format used for a small non-governmental organisation in the Middle East. It could be used elsewhere, and avoids including the more complex information in the 'accumulated fund'. This kind of funds statement, often without accruals and prepayments adjustments included, may be presented with a receipts and payments account.

Note the following differences in presentation.

- The changes in terminology in both statements.
- A combination of all 'office expenses' including 'bad debts'.
- The 'transfer to/from fixed assets fund' is a kind of depreciation. Money is set aside from the 'general fund' to a special 'fixed asset fund'. This reduces the excess of income over expenditure. The amount set aside however may not be represented by a real cash/bank balance, unless a transfer has also been made from the bank account to a special savings account.
- The 'funds statement' is based on balance sheet data, *but it is not intended to balance*.

---

**Lomtaka Health Care Centre**
**INCOME STATEMENT**
**FOR THE PERIOD ENDED 31 DECEMBER (YEAR 1)**

**REVENUES**

| | | |
|---|---|---:|
| Grants | | 700,000 |
| Fees | | 110,734 |
| Other | | 20,023 |
| | Total revenues | 830,757 |

**EXPENSES**

| | | |
|---|---|---:|
| Salaries | | 483,109 |
| Rent | | 96,000 |
| Medical purchases | | 163,001 |
| Office expenses | | 25,597 |
| Travel | | 18,394 |
| Seminars/educational activities | | 6,778 |
| | | 792,879 |
| Transferred to fixed assets fund | | 15,219 |
| | Total expenses | 808,098 |
| Excess of revenues over expenses | | 22,659 |

---

---

### Lomtaka Health Care Centre
### FUNDS STATEMENT
### AS AT 31 DECEMBER (YEAR 1)

**GENERAL FUND**
**Current assets**

| | |
|---|---:|
| Closing stock | 10,129 |
| Accounts receivable | 33,839 |
| Cash and bank | 30,385 |
| | 74,353 |

**Current Liabilities**

| | |
|---|---:|
| Accounts payable | 26,971 |

| | |
|---|---:|
| **Loan** | 10,000 |

**FIXED ASSETS FUND**
**Transferred from general fund**      15,219

---

## EXAMPLE 4

This format of balance sheet is common in countries influenced by the accounting style of the United States of America. It is used in the Caribbean and Central and South America.

Note the following differences in presentation.

- Differences in terminology.
- The order of the assets in the balance sheet. The *least permanent asset*, cash, comes first in the balance sheet.

# Lomtaka Health Care Centre
## STATEMENT OF INCOME AND EXPENDITURE
## FOR THE PERIOD ENDED 31 DECEMBER (YEAR 1)

### INCOME

| | |
|---|---:|
| Grants   - WEV | 100,000 |
|       - Donoraid | 250,000 |
| Department of Health | 350,000 |
| Revenue from service charges | 110,734 |
| Other | 20,023 |
| | 830,757 |

### EXPENSES

| | |
|---|---:|
| Salaries | 483,109 |
| Rent | 96,000 |
| Purchase of drugs | 103,192 |
| Medical supplies | 59,809 |
| Electricity | 11,547 |
| Travelling expenses | 18,394 |
| Seminars | 6,778 |
| Office costs | 10,887 |
| Other payments | 2,192 |
| Depreciation | 15,219 |
| Bad debts and provision | 971 |
| | 808,098 |
| | |
| **Excess of income over expenditure** | **22,659** |

---

### Lomtaka Health Care Centre
### BALANCE SHEET AS AT 31 DECEMBER (YEAR 1)

**ASSETS**

| | | |
|---|---:|---:|
| Cash | | 824 |
| Bank | | 29,561 |
| Payments in advance | | 1,500 |
| Income in arrears | | 10,000 |
| Receivables | | 22,339 |
| Inventory | | 10,129 |
| *Total current assets* | | *74,353* |
| | | |
| Equipment | 30,198 | |
| *less* depreciation | 6,040 | 24,158 |
| | | |
| Vehicle | 15,298 | |
| *less* depreciation | 9,179 | 6,119 |

**TOTAL ASSETS**      **104,630**

**LIABILITIES**

| | |
|---|---:|
| Payables | 13,236 |
| Accruals | 10,185 |
| Income in advance | 3,550 |
| *Total current liabilities* | *26,971* |
| | |
| Accumulated fund | 67,659 |
| | |
| Loan | 10,000 |

**TOTAL LIABILITIES**      **104,630**

---

# Appendix D

## Glossary of Accounting Terms

[Note: *Italics* indicate cross-references within the glossary]

**Acid Test Ratio**
See *Liquidity Ratio*.

**Account**
A record of a number of transactions grouped together by type.

**Account Codes**
A combination of numbers or letters listed in a *chart of accounts* which represent items of *income, expenditure, assets, liabilities* or *accumulated fund*. Codes are frequently used with computerised accounting systems.

**Accountant**
Someone who is qualified (usually by taking exams) to give financial advice.

**Accounting**
The process of recording and using information to prepare *accounting statements* and reports and the interpretation of these and other data.

**Accounting Period**
The period of time covered by a *budget, income and expenditure* or trading or *profit and loss account* (or their equivalent). Externally produced information is often for twelve months.

**Accounting Policies**
The basis on which *accounting statements* are prepared. Policies may cover general accounting principles, or more specific points relating to the organisation.

## Accounting Records
Information kept to record transactions. Examples include the *cash book* and the *ledger*.

## Accounting Statements (or Financial Statements)
Financial summaries produced at the end of an *accounting period*. Examples include a *receipts and payments account*, an *income and expenditure account* and a *balance sheet*.

## Accounts
The *accounting statements* or records prepared which show how money has been used.

## Accruals
*Income* or *expenditure* which is due in an *accounting period*, but not received or paid by the end of the period.

## Accruals Accounting
The basis of accounting where adjustments are made to show the income earned and expenditure incurred during the *accounting period*. See also *Cash Accounting*.

## Accumulated Fund
The value of money used to start an organisation together with *capital grants*, plus previous years' *surpluses* and less previous years' *deficits*.

## Advances Register
A record showing money given to staff for a particular purpose, how it has been accounted for and whether the amount is still outstanding.

## Analysed Cash Book
The record of all cash and/or bank amounts coming in to and going out of an organisation, with additional columns to identify the type of receipt or payment.

## Asset
An item owned by an organisation.

## Audit
An independent assessment of an organisation by a qualified person(s).

**Audit Report**
A written document, signed by an *auditor*, attached to the *accounting statements* at the end of an *accounting period*. It identifies the standards by which the audit has been undertaken and states the *auditors' opinion*. It also discloses any major weaknesses found in the course of the *audit*. See also *Qualified Audit Report* and *Unqualified Audit Report*.

**Auditor(s)**
The person(s) who undertakes an *audit*.

**Auditors' Opinion**
The opinion within an *audit report*, which summarises the *auditors'* view of the organisation.

**Bad Debt**
An outstanding debt which is unlikely to be paid, and may need to be charged against *expenditure*.

**Balance Sheet**
An accounting statement which lists what is owned (assets) and owed (liabilities) at a particular point in time.

**Bank Book**
The record kept to show all items going in to or out of the bank account. Usually known as, and part of, the *cash book*.

**Bank Charge**
An amount charged to a bank account holder by a bank.

**Bank Interest (received)**
An amount paid by a bank to its customer, to compensate for money held in a customer's account and used by the bank. Most often paid on a *deposit* or *savings account*.

**Bank Overdraft**
A bank account with money overspent from a *current account*. This may be a temporary situation whilst the bank account holder is waiting for further funds to be deposited, or by a longer-term agreement with the bank.

## Bank Pass Book
A book provided and updated by a bank to show the record of money held in an account.

## Bank Reconciliation
A method of confirming that an organisation's own *accounting records* agree with that of the bank as shown in the *bank statement* or *bank pass book*.

## Bank Statement
A list produced by a bank showing all entries in an account over a period of time, and the balance held at the end of the period.

## Bookkeeper
A person who keeps the record of accounts and other financial transactions.

## Book-keeping Adjustments
Adjustments to the *accounting records*, to show the effect on items where no money has been received or paid. These are often made at the end of an *accounting period*. Examples include *depreciation*, and *accruals* and *prepayments*.

## Books of Account (or 'The Books')
The *accounting records* kept by an organisation.

## Brought Down (or B/D)
An amount of money included in the *cash book*, or other record as a starting point at the beginning of a new *accounting period*. The same figure would have been shown as a balance *carried down*, at the end of the previous period.

## Brought Forward (or B/F)
A figure included in a *cash book* or other accounting record at the start of a page. The amount is shown at the end of the previous page and described as *carried forward*.

## Budget
A financial plan of an entity relating to a period of time.

## Budget and Actual Statement (or Budget and Actuals)
A statement comparing budgeted *income* and *expenditure* by type with actual *income* and *expenditure*. Differences are known as variances, and are also shown.

**Budget and Actuals**
See *Budget and Actual Statement*.

**Capital (or Capital Account)**
A sum of money invested in a business or organisation by its owner(s).

**Capital Budget**
A budget which includes *capital income* and *capital expenditure*. Examples include a *capital grant*, buildings and equipment.

**Capital Expenditure**
Amounts paid for the purchase of long-term *assets*. Examples include buildings, computers and machinery.

**Capital Grant**
An amount donated to an organisation for its long-term use. Examples include a grant to cover initial start-up costs.

**Capital Income**
Income for long-term use. An example is a *capital grant*.

**Carried Down (or C/D)**
A figure included in the accounts as an amount remaining at the end of an *accounting period*. This will be the same as the balance *brought down* at the beginning of the next period.

**Carried Forward (or C/F)**
A figure included in a *cash book* or *bank book* or other accounting record at the end of a page. The amount is shown at the start of the next page and described as *brought forward*.

**Cash Accounting**
The basis of accounting which shows only *receipts* and *payments* received or paid during the accounting period, with no adjustments. See also *Accruals Accounting*.

**Cash Book**
A record of money coming in to and going out of an organisation in date order. This term is used to include cash and bank transactions.

## Cash Budget (or Cash Flow Forecast)
A statement which forecasts the money coming in to and going out of an organisation over a period of time in the future.

## Cash Flow Forecast
See *Cash Budget*.

## Cashier
The person responsible for administering the cash and bank transactions.

## Chart of Accounts
A list of *account codes* used for a particular organisation.

## Closing Balance
See *Carried Down* and *Carried Forward*.

## Closing Stock
The value of the goods held at the end of an *accounting period*. Calculated as the value of goods held at the beginning of the accounting period (*opening stock*) plus the value of purchases, less the value of goods used during the year.

## Code
See *Account Codes*.

## Cost of Goods Sold
A figure appearing in a commercial *trading account*. It is calculated as *opening stock*, plus *purchases* less *closing stock*.

## Credit (1)
A term used in *double-entry book-keeping* to mean an entry on the right-hand side on an account.

## Credit (2)
An amount which a customer is allowed to pay after the sale of goods or services has taken place.

## Creditors (or Payables)
Those to whom an organisation owes money for goods or services. *Accounting statements* prepared in North or South America often use the word *payables*.

**Current Account**
A bank account into which money can be paid, and against which cheques (and other forms of payment) can be drawn.

**Current Assets**
Amounts which are already cash or bank account items or are likely to be turned into these within the next year. Examples include *stock, debtors,* cash and bank balances.

**Current Liabilities**
Amounts which are due for payment within the next year. Examples include *creditors* and *bank overdrafts.*

**Current Ratio**
A calculation expressing the relationship of current assets to current liabilities.

**Debit**
A term used in *double-entry book-keeping* to mean an entry on the left-hand side of an *account.*

**Debtors (or Receivables)**
Outstanding amounts owed to an organisation for goods or services. *Accounting statements* prepared in North or South America often use the word *receivables.*

**Deficit**
When expenditure is more than *income.* The term is often used in not-for-profit *accounting statements.* See also *Surplus.*

**Deposit Account**
A bank account which gains *interest.* A bank may require a number of days' advance notice for funds to be withdrawn.

**Depreciation**
A method of allocating the cost of a *fixed asset* over the period of time it is likely to be used.

**Designated Funds**
Money identified for a particular purpose by the *governing body.*

### Development organisation
An organisation involved in local, national or international development.

### Donor(s)
Individuals or institutions providing funding or support to *development organisations* and *non-governmental organisations*.

### Double-entry Book-keeping
A way of keeping *accounting records*, each transaction being recorded in two separate *accounts* – one a *debit* the other a *credit*.

### Excess of Expenditure over Income
A figure calculating the *deficit* made in an *accounting period*.

### Excess of Income over Expenditure
A figure calculating the *surplus* made in an *accounting period*.

### Expenditure
Amounts which have been or are due to be paid.

### External Audit
An *audit* undertaken by an independent person or group of people not employed by the organisation being audited. See also *Internal Audit*.

### Final Accounting Statements or Accounting Statements, or Financial Statements
The *income and expenditure* or *profit and loss account* (or their equivalent) together with a balance sheet, drawn up at the end of an accounting period.

### Financial Audit
An examination of financial records and *accounting statements*. See also *Management Audit*.

### Financial Controls
See *Internal Controls*.

### Financial Report
See *Budget and Actual Statement*.

### Financial Statements (or Accounting Statements)
Financial summaries produced at the end of an *accounting period*. Examples include a *receipts and payments account*, an *income and expenditure account* and a *balance sheet*.

### Fixed Assets
Items held for more than one year. Examples include buildings, vehicles and computers.

### Fixed Assets Register
A list of *fixed assets* and *depreciation* calculations updated each year. See also *Inventory*.

### Float
An amount of money allocated to be used for an unspecified purpose. An example is money allocated for use as *petty cash*.

### Fund Accounting
A system of accounting to ensure money donated for a particular purpose is so applied.

### Governing Body
The group of individuals legally responsible for an organisation.

### Gross Profit
*Profit* earned from trading before expenses are deducted.

### Guaranteed Budget
The *budget* based on income guaranteed at the time it is planned, in terms of contingency planning.

### Historical Cost Convention
An accounting principle stating that items included in the accounts are usually included at the original cost. If this is not the case, a *note to the accounts* will say so.

### Honorary Auditor
An *auditor* who either is not paid or is paid only a nominal amount for his/her services.

## Income
Money received or due to be received.

## Income and Expenditure Account
A statement showing money received and paid out during an *accounting period*, together with *book-keeping adjustments* for items such as *depreciation*, *accruals* and *prepayments*. This is the equivalent of a *profit and loss account* used in a commercial business.

## Income in Advance
An amount received before it was due.

## Income in Arrears
An amount that is due but has not yet been received.

## Inflation
An increase in prices.

## Insolvent
An inability to pay outstanding debts.

## Interest
An amount added when money is held and used by someone else, for example a bank.

## Interim Audit
An *audit* conducted prior to and as part of the final (year end) audit.

## Internal Audit
An *audit* undertaken by a person(s) who is employed by the organisation being audited. See also *External Audit*.

## Internal Controls
The procedures adopted to ensure accurate accounting and to prevent the possibility of misappropriation.

## Inventory (1)
An amount of stock.

## Inventory (2)
A record of *fixed assets* held.

**Investment Account**
See *Savings Account*.

**Invoice**
A written request for payment for goods or services.

**Journal**
A record of transfers between different *accounts* in a *ledger*.

**Ledger**
A record of the *account* transactions during a particular period.

**Letter of Engagement**
An agreement between an *auditor* and the organisation being audited, stating the scope of the *audit* and other practical details.

**Liability**
An amount owed.

**Limiting Factor**
The reason why additional budgeting *objectives* cannot be achieved. An example is insufficient money.

**Liquidity**
The availability of cash (or other *current assets* which are easily turned into cash) to meet payments due.

**Liquidity Ratio (or Acid Test Ratio)**
A calculation expressing the relationship of *current assets* (excluding *stock*) to *current liabilities*.

**Loan**
An amount borrowed for a fixed period. An example is a bank loan.

**Long-Term Liabilities**
Amounts owed that will become due for payment in twelve months or more.

**Loss**
Excess of expenses over earnings. See also *Profit*.

## Management Audit
An examination of an organisation's management and financial processes and systems. See also *Financial Audit.*

## Management Letter
A letter identifying outstanding points and recommendations, sent to an organisation from the *auditor* at the end of an *audit.*

## Net Book Value
The value of an *asset* after *depreciation* to date, shown in the *balance sheet.*

## Net Profit
Earnings less all expenses.

## Net Realisable Value
The value that would be obtained from the sale of *stock*, less any costs of selling.

## Non-governmental Organisation (NGO)
A not-for-profit body involved in local, national or international development.

## Note(s) to the Accounts
Additional information regarding the calculation of figures within *accounting statements*, or principles adopted in their compilation.

## Objectives
The stated aims of an organisation.

## Opening Balance
See *Brought Down* and *Carried Down.*

## Opening Stock
The value of goods held at the beginning of an *accounting period.*

## Optimal Budget
The programme that would be undertaken given that the most favourable amount of funding were available, in terms of contingency planning.

## Overdraft
An amount which a bank allows to be temporarily overspent from a current account.

**Payables**
See *Creditors*.

**Payment voucher**
A request for payment signed by an authorised member of staff.

**Payments**
Money going out of an organisation.

**Payments in Advance**
See *Prepayments*.

**Petty Cash**
A cash amount held by a person not keeping the *cash book*. It is used for small *purchases* and reimbursed from the main *cash book*.

**Prepayments (or Payments in Advance)**
Amounts relating to a future *accounting period* which have already been paid.

**Profit**
Excess of earnings over expenses. See also *Loss*.

**Profit and Loss Account**
An *accounting statement* showing a commercial business's earnings, expenses and *net profit* for a particular *accounting period*.

**Provision for doubtful debts**
An amount charged as *expenditure* to cover possible future non-payment of outstanding *debtors*.

**Purchases**
Goods and services bought either for resale or for use in the current *accounting period*.

**Qualified Audit Report**
An *auditor's opinion* showing a negative comment about an organisation being audited. See also *Unqualified Audit Report*.

**Ratio Analysis**
A technique for comparing items in the *accounting statements* with the *budget*, previous years and other similar organisations.

### Receipt

A numbered piece of paper giving details of an amount of money received or paid. It shows the amount of the transaction, its purpose and the signature of the person receiving the money.

### Receipts

Money coming in to an organisation.

### Receipts and Payments Account

A summary of bank and cash items coming in to and going out of an organisation over a period of time (with no adjustments).

### Receivables

See *Debtors*.

### Reducing Balance Method of Depreciation

A way of depreciating, using a fixed percentage. The previous year's *net book value* is multiplied by the percentage to calculate the current year's *depreciation* charge.

### Reserves

The amount of the previous years' *surpluses* or *profits* remaining.

### Residual Value

Estimated value of an *asset* at the end of its useful life.

### Restricted Funds

Money received from a *donor* and held for a particular purpose. See also *Unrestricted Funds*.

### Revenue Budget

A *budget* statement for one year which excludes *capital income* and *capital expenditure* items.

### Revenue Expenditure

Expenditure relating to the current *accounting period* only. Examples include rent and salaries.

### Revenue Income

Income relating to the current *accounting period* only. Examples include fees and charges.

**Savings Account (or Investment Account)**
A bank account which adds *interest* to the money invested.

**Segregation of Duties**
The system of dividing work so that one person does not process every aspect of an entire transaction. The aim is to prevent errors and misappropriation.

**'Signed off'**
After the completion of the *accounting statements* and the *audit*, the accounts are literally signed by the *auditor* and a representative of the organisation being audited.

**Stock**
See *Closing Stock* and *Opening Stock*.

**Straight Line Method of Depreciation**
This *depreciation* charge is calculated by taking the cost price of an asset less the *residual value* at the end of its life (if any), and dividing the result by the number of years the item is expected to last. The most common method of calculating depreciation.

**Surplus**
The amount remaining after reducing *income* by *expenditure*. The term is often used in not-for-profit *accounting statements*. See also *Deficit*.

**Survival Budget**
The minimum budget required to keep existing programmes going, in terms of contingency planning.

**Tender**
Written quote for the provision of goods or services at a fixed price.

**Total Depreciation to Date**
The amount of *depreciation* charged from the purchase of an *asset* to the current date.

**Trading Account**
An *accounting* statement measuring *gross profit*, taking sales less the *cost of goods sold*, but ignoring expenses. It either precedes, or is part of a *profit and loss account*.

### Trial Balance
A summary of the balances from each *account* of the *ledger*, shown in two separate columns of *debits* and *credits*. If the total of each column agrees with the other, the *ledger* balances.

### Unqualified Audit Report
A standard *audit report* expressing the *auditor's opinion* of an organisation, but without any additional negative comments. See also *Qualified Audit Report*.

### Unrestricted Funds
Money available that can be used for any item of *expenditure* within an organisation. See also *Restricted Funds*.

### Variance
The difference between budgeted and actual *income* or *expenditure*.

### Variance Report
See *Budget* and *Actual Statement*.

### Virement
Movement of an amount from one budget item to another.

### Voucher
A document supporting entries in the accounts. Examples include *receipts* and *invoices*.

### Working Budget
What is realistically expected to happen in the *revenue budget*, in terms of contingency planning.

### Working Capital
The amount of *current assets* less *current liabilities* held and used in day-to-day activities.

### Zero-Based Budgeting
Preparing a *budget* using the current year's *objectives* as a starting point. The assumption being that, initially there is no commitment to spend on any item. An alternative is using last year's figures and adjusting by an agreed percentage.

# Books Linking Financial Management and International Development

Cammack, J., *Basic Accounting for Small Groups*, Oxford: Oxfam, 1992.

Collins, R., *Management Controls for Development Organisations Parts 1 and 2*, Crediton: Stephen Sims and Partners, 1994.

Denis, P., and Ogara, W., *Financial Accountability Guidelines*, Nairobi: Corat (Africa), 1992.

Dickson, D.E.N. (ed.), *Improve Your Business Handbook*, Geneva: International Labour Office, 1986.

Dickson, D.E.N. (ed.), *Improve Your Business Workbook*, Geneva: International Labour Office, 1986.

Eade, D., and Williams S. (eds.), *The Oxfam Manual for Development and Relief: Volume 1*, Oxford: Oxfam, 1995.

Elliott, N., *Basic Accounting for Credit and Savings Schemes*, Oxford: Oxfam, 1996.

Kandasami, M., *Governance and Financial Management in Non-Profit Organisations*, New Delhi: Caritas India, 1997.

PRIA, *Manual on Financial Management and Account Keeping*, New Delhi: Society for Participatory Research in Asia, 1991.

Shapiro, J., *Financial Management for Self-reliance*, Durban: Olive Publications, 1995.

Vincent, F., *Manual of Practical Management of Third World Rural Development Associations, Volume 2: Financial Management*, London: Intermediate Technology Publications, 1997.

# Index